The
Ó Súilleabháin
Manuscripts

by

Dr. Thomas S. Smith, Sr.

Dedicated to

All the **front-liners** and **essentials** during the coronavirus pandemic;

in other words, to all those who went out to work

while I remained at home!

ACKNOWLEDGEMENTS

Special Thanks

Sue Smith

Gabriel G. Bell

Keith Chatelain

Julius P. Guillot

Sean Payton and New Orleans Saints Superbowl Team

Carla Moreau

George "Jeff" Franklin, Jr.

Mona Bullard

Paige Smith

"Education don't come by bumping against the schoolhouse."—African-American Proverb

"We are just an advanced breed of monkeys on a minor planet of a very average star."—Stephen Hawking

"In 100 years we have gone from teaching Latin and Greek in high school to teaching Remedial English in college." —Joseph Sobran

"What I did have was incentive. I did not accept my poverty status as the final verdict on a young life."—Cal Thomas

The Ó Súilleabháin Manuscripts

PREFACE

The naming of this collection of writings I have penned over time caused much debate in my mind and much research trying to come up with a title that had not been used before or a title not too close in name to other works. I finally selected **The Ó Súilleabháin Manuscripts** for several reasons: I possess a chunk of Irish DNA as does my sweet wife. My middle name is Sullivan. I have a redheaded daughter. I have a central character with the name of O Suilleabhain in my Civil War *Just a Piece of Red String* novel series.

I hope you find some interesting and entertaining writing and some that can reveal to you some insights about my teaching and my outlook on life.

A Vision Once I Saw

Ken remembered seeing her yesterday, September 3, 1989, at the International Bazaar; in fact, she was leaning against one of the huge columns of the lacquer-red Japanese Torii welcoming gate. He had thought it unusual that someone so pretty was there alone, just seeming to be waiting and watching for no one in particular. It was the look on her face. In the second or two he glanced at her, he drew the conclusion that she was perplexed and forlorn.

He had continued walking and conversing with his companions. His attention turned to the exotic shops from around the world found in the International Bazaar there in Freeport on Grand Bahama Island. The shops had some of everything it seemed. Oriental embroidered robes, shining brass works, carved ivory, antique swords, silver jewelry, crystal, rare shells, books, and worldwide food specialties were just a few of the things that impressed Ken. He had been outside the United States before and wasn't easily impressed, but all of this in one marketplace was fantastic. Ken had put the young woman out of his memory.

But here she was again. Here on the beach. Alone. Again. He was going to walk right in front of her.

She sat on a beach towel spread out on the white sand. The shallow, crystal-clear water was fifteen to twenty feet from her. Ken, strolling in the edge of the water, would pass right in front of her. Since she was staring out toward the open water, she would have to see him as he passed. Ken slowed his already leisurely pace.

There was something about her, maybe something about him—his curiosity concerning the pretty young woman being alone—that made him want to speak to her, to get to know her. It wasn't eight o'clock yet when he had left the hotel this morning to seek a time to be alone himself, a time to think about his future. He had thought that a relaxing walk along the beach was just what he needed. It would be a time of uncluttered thinking and planning.

Perhaps that was why she was there, too. Just to think. Just to be alone for a while. But she was alone yesterday. He had seen that.

Ken was closer now. She didn't even turn her head to glance at him as he approached. Ken surmised that she was lost in thought or just basking in the beauty and serenity of a deserted beach.

The young woman wore a bikini. The bottom piece was cut high on the sides, and the top tied behind her back. The swimsuit was a bright red. She wore wide-rimmed sunglasses that had a reddish tint. Her shining black hair was topped by a visor-cap proclaiming, "It's Better in the Bahamas!" She had a dark tan.

Ken's mind jammed with thoughts of his being brash and speaking to her, of his introducing himself and being judged rude, and of his being friendly and merely saying, "Good morning." Ken wasn't one to be where he wasn't wanted.

He was only a few paces before walking directly in front of her gaze when, unbelievingly, he heard himself say, "Hi. I'm Ken Harrell. Isn't the beach here great? I saw you yesterday at the Bazaar. What's your name?" He stopped and stood still, the clear water lapping on and over his feet and ankles.

Slowly the young woman directed her gaze at Ken. She remained silent. He wished he could see her eyes, but her sunglasses prevented it. He took a step toward her; she still said nothing.

Ken smiled at her, and she smiled back. He relaxed.

"I'm Heather. Heather McBrighton. You're an American?"

"Yes," said Ken. "From Texas. How about you?"

"I'm from Florida," she responded. They talked for a short time about The Bahamas—the shops, the beach, the people.

Ken said, "You know, Heather, I almost didn't say anything to you. I almost walked on by. But something made me blurt out those first words. I guess that you just seemed so—so alone. Am I right or wrong?"

Heather removed her sunglasses, and Ken saw a heavy sadness in her eyes. A tear formed in the middle of one eye and ran quickly down her left cheek.

"I'm right," said Ken, and he sat beside her. "You want to talk about it? Tell me. Sometimes it helps to talk. I know I'm a stranger, but maybe that's good." He paused. He looked directly at her eyes. She returned the look and then stood. She reached out her hand to him.

"Walk with me," Heather implored.

Ken gathered her beach towel and took her hand. They went to the water's edge and turned to walk along the beach. For a couple of minutes, neither said anything. Heather released Ken's hand and began to talk as they slowly walked.

"My father and mother have recently finished an ugly divorce proceeding. I'm here with my father. We're staying at the Xanadu Beach Hotel," she related.

"The Xanadu," he echoed.

"Yes," Heather stated and paused and then said, "In Xanadu did Kubla Khan a stately pleasure dome decree . . ." Her voice trailed off.

"I've heard that before. Isn't it from a poem?"

Heather continued, "It is. By Coleridge. The line fits my father. He thinks he can decree pleasure for me, like this vacation. He and my mother are trying to buy my love, so that I'll love one of them more than the other. Both give me expensive gifts and lots of money. Now that the divorce is final, they are trying to outbid each other for their daughter. It's so stupid. They don't realize that I love both of them—no matter what. It's all so crazy. Every time they get together, they're at each other's throat. I'm caught in the middle. I hate how they act. They make me feel so bad. It would be better if I weren't around." She cried as they walked.

"All of that's not your fault. You can't blame yourself for their problems, for the divorce," Ken said.

They continued walking, silent now for a time.

"But that's not all. I didn't tell you about . . . about . . . ." Heather stopped suddenly and plopped down into the shallow water. She choked back tears.

Ken touched her left hand, then held it firmly in his hands. "About what?" he asked gently.

"Kathy. Kathy and the accident." She hesitated. "The accident. Kathy was killed in a car wreck. I was driving. I killed her. I killed Kathy. She was my best friend—like a sister. It was my fault," Heather blurted out the words. She cried even more intensely.

"Take it easy, Heather. Take it easy," Ken said soothingly. "I'm sure it wasn't your fault. Your said it was an accident." He had kneeled in the water beside her.

Now Heather clung to him. She was shaking. Ken consoled her. In a few minutes they stood and walked from the water over the sand to the shade of a group of trees. They sat, arms around one another.

Heather ceased crying and shaking. Still she said nothing. Ken didn't know what to say, so he just held her.

After a while Heather looked up at Ken and said, "I'm all right now. Let's go back."

"Sure," Ken replied. "I'll walk you back to the hotel."

"You're a nice guy, Ken. Will you be my friend?"

"I already am."

Heather put her arm around Ken's waist, and they walked on in the sand. They talked about music and cars and food. Heather laughed when Ken made jokes and acted silly on the way back.

The two young people decided to have lunch together. At the hotel Heather went up to her room to change clothes while Ken remained in the lobby to telephone his traveling companions.

Over lunch they made plans for the afternoon. They rented a boat and went off to be together, to be young, to be happy. The beautiful beaches and sparkling waters were what the young man and the young woman needed to cement their newly formed friendship. Heather was light-hearted all afternoon. Not once did she mention her parents or Kathy.

The day was drawing to a close when Ken turned the boat back toward Freeport. The island was beautiful even at this time. They turned in the boat and walked hand-in-hand toward Heather's hotel.

She was talking about how much fun she had on their little excursion. She babbled ceaselessly. Ken had enjoyed the day and his new friend, too. He hoped that he had lightened her burden somewhat. He was glad that she was happy.

They were walking, looking up at the Xanadu Hotel, and saying how pretty it was at night. Without warning, Heather pulled Ken over to the edge of the walkway where the light was dim.

Heather reached up and kissed Ken. "Thanks for a fun day. You're not a stranger any more, like you were this morning. I don't know why I told you all I did. I must have needed someone to talk to. I needed you, Ken."

"You're a fun person. You are lovely, witty, and sweet."

"Thanks," replied Heather. "I'll have to find my father and spend the rest of the evening with him and his friends. I'm late already, but I don't care."

They walked on to the hotel, chatting idly about the people they saw and passed. In the lobby Heather turned to Ken and asked, "What are we going to do tomorrow? You want to go back to the beach in the morning? I'll tell Daddy about you, and we can spend all day together—even tomorrow night. I'll get—"

"Wait. Hold on a minute," Ken said. "I'd love to spend all day, even all week with you. But . . . "

"But what?"

Ken placed his hands on Heather's shoulders and looked directly into her blue eyes and said in a low, apologetic tone, "But tomorrow I must leave. I must return to Texas to school. My plane departs at seven-thirty in the morning. I'm sorry."

Heather was speechless. She was stunned. She just stared, wide-eyed, at Ken.

"Hey, girl. I'm sorry. But I have to go. I have to leave tomorrow."

"Why didn't you tell me? Why didn't you say that you must leave tomorrow?"

"I tried a couple of times, but I just could not bring myself to tell you. I didn't want to spoil our good time," replied Ken.

"I told you everything. I bared my soul to you. I thought you were special. You seemed so great."

"I'm still the same person. I haven't changed just because tomorrow I must leave The Bahamas," said Ken. "I like you, Heather. We had fun. We still can. Can't you talk with your father? Don't you think he'd let you be with me tonight?"

Heather just looked at Ken. Turning suddenly, she said, "Good-bye, Ken. It was fun today," as she hurried away.

"Heather! Heather! Come back! Let's talk!"

She disappeared among a group of people. Ken stood there. He took a few steps forward.

"She's gone," said Ken to himself. He took a couple of steps and stopped again. He paused, not knowing what to do. "She didn't tell me her room number."

Then he turned quickly and walked briskly to the registration desk. A worker there greeted him cheerily and asked, "May I help you, sir?"

"Yes, I think you can," replied Ken. "What room is Heather McBrighton staying in?"

"Let me see, sir." The clerk moved to a computer.

Ken waited, anxious to know the room number so that he could talk with Heather. He didn't want her to be upset with him. His fingertips rapped on the counter top.

"You said the McBrighton party, sir?"

"Yes, Heather McBrighton, specifically."

"Mr. McBrighton requested that no information be given out. I'm sorry."

"But I must know. It's important. Heather just left me crying. She's upset. I must talk with her," said Ken, exasperated.

"I'm sorry, but hotel policy prevents my giving out that information. Perhaps she'll call or visit you, sir," the clerk said.

"But she doesn't know where I'm staying."

"May I make a suggestion? Why don't you leave your name and hotel here. Miss McBrighton may check here to see if you inquired about her," said the clerk.

Ken gave the information and left immediately for his hotel. He sat in his room, looked out the window at the beach and blue water, and thought about Heather. When his companions asked him to go out for a last-night celebration, he refused. He waited. He paced the floor. He brooded over Heather. He worried. He didn't understand why this was happening—why he was bothered so much by the situation.

Ken lay on the bed. He thought about first seeing Heather, about talking with her and being with her. She was special. He wished she would call him.

He got up and started packing for his morning departure for home. He couldn't get Heather off his mind.

His friends came back after midnight. One came in to talk for a while. He left after twenty minutes.

Ken tried to sleep, but he tossed and turned for a couple of hours. It seemed longer. The next thing he knew he was awakened by the ringing of the phone. It was one of his friends checking to see if he was up and preparing to leave for the airport.

They checked out of the hotel and were driven to the airport. It was six forty-five. Ken looked for Heather everywhere. She knew when he was to leave. He could wait only a short while longer. He looked out at the planes. He turned around to go out to board his plane.

Heather meekly said, "Hi, Ken. I'm sorry." There she was, standing only a few feet from him.

"I tried to see you, to get your room number. But the hotel wouldn't let me," blurted out Ken.

"Let me talk before you have to get aboard the plane," said Heather as they walked.

He nodded his assent.

"I won't be a problem for my parents," Heather continued. "I know what is what now. I thought about everything after I left you yesterday."

"Heather," Ken interrupted.

She reached up to put her fingers gently on his lips to quiet him. "I know what you are trying to say. I've got everything straight." She smiled at Ken.

Heather reached into the pocket of her sundress and withdrew a small box. She opened it and held it up for Ken to see.

"It's an initial ring for you. To remember me by. Do you like it?"

"Yes. Thank you. You didn't need to do that."

"Yes, I did. It's for you. From me. We had a special time together," Heather said.

"Let me get your address. I'll write," Ken injected. "We may get to see each other again."

Heather drew a small folded piece of paper from her pocket and put it into the ring box and closed the top. As she put the box into Ken's hand, she said, "I've written everything on the paper in the ring box. Good-bye, Ken. Don't worry about me. I won't be a problem for anyone anymore."

Heather reached up to kiss Ken.

Heather turned and quickly went away. Ken watched her move away. She had had that look in her eyes when she kissed him—that forlorn, detached, lonely look. But it had been different in a way, too. There was a certain calmness.

But Ken didn't have time to stand there and ponder. He had to hurry to the plane. He was late. He walked briskly and boarded the plane. He was the last one to board. His friends teased him about it.

Ken settled into his less-than-comfortable seat and thought about Heather. The plane began to taxi onto the runway to position itself for takeoff. He hadn't fastened his seatbelt yet. The stewardess reminded him. He reached to do so. He still held the ring box. He buckled the belt. The plane was motionless. He knew takeoff would be momentarily.

He opened the ring box to look again at the ring. The small piece of paper fluttered out. He caught it and unfolded it. He looked intently. On the paper was no address. On it were these sentences.

"Ken. Thanks. You're a sweet guy. You care about people. I'm glad we met and spent time together. You're special. Don't concern yourself about me. I've figured everything out. I won't be a problem for anyone <u>anymore</u>. Good-bye. Good-bye.   Heather"

"My God!" exclaimed Ken in a loud voice. "She's going to kill herself. Let me off this plane!"

Ken unbuckled his seatbelt as the plane's engines began pushing the plane forward. He stood, attracting the attention of the flight attendants. He moved toward the doorway of the plane.

"Let me off! I must get back to her hotel! Stop the plane!"

Three flight attendants and Ken's companions tried to calm Ken. The plane had stopped dead on the runway. An attendant had alerted the pilot and the other crew members.

It took thirty minutes for Ken to get off the plane and begin to head for the hotel. A police officer drove him there. It seemed to him to take forever to get to Heather's hotel. He rushed to the registration desk and screamed out his problem. Security guards and the manager were summoned.

"She's going to kill herself! She could be dying right now," Ken shouted in anger at those who were restraining him. He held the note in his hand out to the manager and screamed for him to look at it.

The manager, now realizing the situation, got the room number and directed the security guards and Ken to the elevators. They made it to Heather's floor and raced down the hall. The manager and Ken banged on the door. No response. Then the manager inserted his pass key and turned it. Ken barged into the room and found Heather lying on the bed. Blood, flowing from her left wrist, had stained the bedding. She was unconscious.

Heather's wrist was wrapped to stop the bleeding, and she was picked up by one of the security guards and Ken and rushed to Rand Memorial Hospital.

At the hospital, medical personnel took over, and Ken was made to stay in a waiting area. He paced. He questioned himself as to why he had not realized what Heather was going to do when she had spoken with him before he boarded the plane. He thought himself so stupid, so blind, so unfeeling. He sat, placing his head in his hands. "Please, God," he prayed, "save her." He repeated this over and over.

A man rushed through the waiting area and inquired about Heather at the nurses' station just down the corridor. Ken thought that the man must be Heather's father. He could not hear the conversation. A few minutes later the man came toward Ken.

The two introduced themselves and talked about Heather. Mr. McBrighton thanked Ken for what he had done. They talked intensely about Heather. Ken explained what he knew and what he thought. Heather's father was both amazed and dismayed at what Ken told him. He broke down and cried, promising to correct things for his daughter if she came out of this tragedy alive.

They sat in silence for a long time.

A doctor approached them. "Mr. McBrighton?"

"Yes. Here," said Heather's father. Both he and Ken stood nervously. The doctor smiled.

"She will be fine. Please sit down and let me explain," he said.

The doctor told them that Heather had lost a lot of blood and probably would have died had she not been discovered and rushed to the hospital. He also told them that once they thought Heather was gone.

Her heart had stopped beating, and all vital signs had been lost for several minutes. The doctors had been able to revive her. He didn't seem to understand exactly how they did it. He implied that God apparently intervened in Heather's favor.

Heather couldn't be seen for another hour or so. She would be moved to a private room. Then they and a nurse could sit with her.

Ken found a phone and made a few calls to explain where he was and why. When he had finished, he was told that Heather was in her room and could be seen. He went there and sat beside her bed with Mr. McBrighton.

The nurse stayed for two hours and then left, checking Heather every twenty minutes.

A few minutes after three o'clock Heather stirred. Ken got up and leaned over her. Mr. McBrighton had stepped out for a moment to try to telephone Heather's mother again.

Ken looked at Heather's face. He leaned over and gently kissed her forehead. He drew back. Heather's eyes opened. With amazement, she whispered, "Ken." Her eyes closed. She slept again.

Heather's father made arrangements for Ken to stay at the hotel and finally persuaded Ken to leave the hospital at midnight to go rest. Mr. McBrighton stayed at the hospital at Heather's bedside.

Ken slept until after eight. He hurried to the hospital. When he entered the room after knocking on the door, he saw Heather's father standing by the bed, gently holding his daughter's hand. Both father and daughter smiled at him. He went over to Heather and kissed her cheek lightly.

"Thank you, Ken, for coming back for me. You saved my life."

Mr. McBrighton explained that Heather was still weak, but the doctor said that her recovery was remarkable. She needed rest, however. Her mother had arrived during the night and was now at the hotel

A few minutes passed. While Heather rested, Mr. McBrighton and Ken went out into the corridor. They talked.

"She seems happy," said Ken. "That's unusual for people who have tried to commit suicide and failed, isn't it?"

"That's what the doctor noticed and said, too," replied Mr. McBrighton. "But Heather has always been unpredictable." He paused. "And this morning she told me of an unbelievable experience."

"What?"

"I'll let her tell you. She made me promise. She'll tell you later when she's stronger," said Heather's father.

That afternoon Heather was stronger and talkative. Ken went in after lunch to spend the afternoon with her.

He sat by her. He placed his hand on the bedrail. She reached to touch his fingers.

"Ken, let me tell you what happened to me in the operating room. The experience has changed me. I know now how stupid I was to try to take my life. I won't ever do it again. I know better now."

"Go ahead, Heather. Tell me."

"I remember watching my blood flow from my wrist and thinking what a beautiful color it was. I stared at what I had done for a while, and then everything just went dark.

The next time I was aware of anything I realized that I was seeing doctors and nurses frantically working over somebody. It was as though I was watching a television program, and the camera was over the operating table. Then I saw who was on the table. I was. There was my body. But I wasn't in it! I felt as if I were floating just above the nurses and doctors. I didn't feel any pain. I heard the people talking about no heartbeat and trying to save me. I saw them redouble their efforts.

I sensed an urge to leave where I was. Somehow I moved out and into the waiting area where Daddy and you were. I saw Daddy crying and you praying silently. And you both were caring about me!

Suddenly I was propelled upward and out of the hospital. I was up above the hospital and other buildings. Now I was moving slowly, very slowly upward as if by design. I could see the entire island. It was so green! I could see the light-blue and dark-blue waters surrounding the island. It was so beautiful! I could see other islands in the distance. It was spectacular! I sensed the beauty and splendor of the Earth. I felt a sense of belonging.

The stars whizzed past me, and then I found myself in a dimly lit tunnel. I felt an urgency to reach the other end, but it was so far away! I seemed to be walking toward the other end. I could tell that a brilliant source of light was outside the end of the tunnel. I was drawn toward it. I was obsessed with it—with getting there.

It seemed that something or someone entered the tunnel from the other end. It happened again and again. I made out forms. They were human in shape. In an instant they were there in front of me.

The first was an older man. I didn't know him, but he reminded me of Daddy. He called me by name and said some other words—all with a Scottish accent.

Then my attention focused on the next figure. It was my grandmother who had died ten years ago. She smiled at me, and I felt warm and loved—just the way I used to feel when I was a little girl sitting on her lap.

I turned, and there was Kathy! I felt her embrace me without touching me. I knew that she didn't blame me for the accident. She didn't say a single word, but I knew—I just knew!

I was closer to the other end of the tunnel and the light source. I sensed a great presence. The light was dazzling. The presence was enlightening and inspiring. I felt a sense of serenity and peace and knowledge. I was almost at the end of the tunnel. I felt the presence cease summoning me. I felt a sense of fulfillment and awe. I sensed that I did not belong there any longer.

Slowly at first and then rapidly I was projected backward through the tunnel and downward toward the Earth. As I exited the tunnel, I saw a young woman playing some type of musical instrument and singing a sweet song. I was back in the hospital, hovering over my motionless body that was still surrounded by the medical personnel. And then I remembered nothing else until I felt someone kiss my forehead. I saw you. I tried to say your name, but I don't know if I did. The next thing I remember was awakening here in this room."

"Your experience is fantastic. I've heard and read about other people having out-of-body experiences like yours. It's amazing," said Ken.

The door to the hospital room opened, and in came Mrs. McBrighton. She was carrying a book. After kissing Heather and being introduced to Ken, she opened the book to a page with a bookmark. She looked at Heather and said, "Here's what you asked for. Coleridge's poem 'Kubla Khan,' right?"

"Ken, will you hold the book for me?" asked Heather as she nodded to her mother.

"Yes, of course," replied Ken. He moved closer as he took the opened book from Heather's mother. They looked at the facing pages. On them was the poem "Kubla Khan."

"There. There it is," said Heather as she pointed to a particular stanza. She read aloud, "A damsel with a dulcimer/In a vision once I saw." She was there at the entrance of the tunnel when I was returning to the hospital.

"Was she?" asked her dad.

Heather read again as they looked at the page and followed.

"A damsel with a dulcimer
In a vision once I saw;
It was an Abyssinian maid,
And on her dulcimer she played,
Singing of Mount Abora.
Could I revive within me
Her symphony and song,
To such a deep delight 'twould win me,"
Heather stopped.

"I have that deep delight now," she said. She cried. "I was stupid before. I won't be like that again. I know better now. Thank you all for caring about me and loving me."

Mr. and Mrs. McBrighton were crying, too. Ken was moved. The others were smiling through their tears.

Heather looked up at Ken and smiled. Her face would never have a lonely, forlorn look again. He was sure of that.

Spring's Eternal Hope

"Ah, no winter of discontent for open minds in the classroom:

Ideas and concepts and understandings germinating and growing,

Axiology alive and rationalizing

In Malthusian proportions.

Of Shakespearean human consequential ramifications

Penetrating Maginot and Mannerheim defensive arguments

With ecumenical dynamism and barbaric enthusiasm.

Utilizing telescopes and microscopes

Underscored by pedagogy and reflection,

Measured algebraically with proper functions of geometric proofs,"

Thought Mrs. Barrett, Mr. Kotter, Mr. Holland, Mrs. Dove,

    Mrs. Crabtree . . .

Confessions of a Semi-Literate Antiquarian

"The future is always beginning now," said Mark Strand. As teachers preparing our students for future literate lives, we must do what our best teachers did for us: teach the "basics plus" in every subject, demand academic excellence, nurture critical thinking skills, instill the idea of lifelong learning, and preach the value of flexibility and acceptance of change. I attempt to do the same plus some lagniappe for the future teachers I teach. Yes, my specialty field is education; I have an undergraduate minor in English. But I did teach English and social studies in public high school in Louisiana and was an administrator in five public schools and a district office. Louisiana students and Michigan students have commonalities with each other and with students throughout the United States. A student is a student in certain respects. I offer a unique informal perspective on the topic of preparing our students to lead literate lives and some additional food for thought.

I submit for your perusal these ideas from the antiquated mind of an old-fashioned teacher who began his professional teaching career in 1971. To look into the future, this teacher must look into the past. "The farther backward you can look, the farther forward you are likely to see," stated Winston Churchill. I think that is pertinent to this topic of future literacy. My teachers, from elementary through high school, demanded quality work from me and the other students. I was not coddled; I was not rewarded for participation or just trying. I learned by working and putting forth effort to learn. I was expected to be an active learner. I was expected to master content. "Hold on," you say! "Knowledge is of two kinds. We know a subject ourselves, or we know where we can find information on it." This observation is not one from the Twenty-First Century. It is from Samuel Johnson. We can look it up, can't we? Of course, Internet is alive and well in the hands of many of us. We have all kinds of "Apps." Some of us can and do look up information we need and use, but I must yield to Samuel Johnson once again because he also can be quoted as having said, "Mankind have a great aversion to intellectual labor; but even supposing knowledge to be easily attainable, more people would be content to be ignorant than would take even a little trouble to acquire it." But even Albert Einstein cautions us when he said, "Information is not knowledge."

We teachers must teach the basics, the basic blocks of information, in all subject areas. We teachers must know our content in order to teach our students. We must teach the fundamentals, but we must go beyond the basics with our students. We cannot stop with the basics; we must insist on more. We teachers must challenge our students to advance as far into a subject as they can. To teach our students to lead literate lives, we must teach by example. We must be literate in everything we teach, even if we are elementary teachers who teach all subjects. We must teach by example as well as by formal instruction.

My teachers demanded excellence. Even from the lesser academically inclined students, my teachers demanded their best. We teachers must demand academic excellence from our students of today. We must instill the pursuit of excellence in our students. We must instill the pursuit of excellence not just for rewards but for achieving excellence in itself.

We teachers must nurture critical thinking skills in our students. My teachers did. They taught me how to learn. They accomplished that impossible mission without my knowing it. Perhaps that is how effective teachers do it. Goethe advanced the thought: "Knowing is not enough; we must apply. Willing is not enough; we must do." Did my teachers study Goethe? Another quotation comes to mind. Alvin Toffler postulated, "The illiterate of the future will not be the person who cannot read. It will be the person who does not know how to learn." Now I know that my teachers never even heard of Toffler! How did they do that?

Instilling the idea and practice of lifelong learning is another monumental task my teachers accomplished during my schooling. "The future is purchased by the present," advised Samuel Johnson. My teachers did not just teach me: they gave me a gift, the gift enabling me to become a lifelong learner and the ability to meet the future in a fearless and opportunistic manner. We teachers must do the same for our students. We must inform our students to take heed of another Alvin Toffler quotation, "Technology feeds on itself. Technology makes more technology possible." Our students must be cognizant of this fact; they must be ready for unimaginable developments in technology. Our students must know that technology can bring them information, but they must understand that information and use it intelligently. We must teach them how to understand, how to analyze, how to apply, and how to capitalize upon the exponentially exploding mass of information.

My teachers promoted the value of flexibility and the acceptance of change as a natural occurrence in life. These ideas bring to mind another quotation from Alvin Toffler, "Change is not merely necessary to life—it is life." My teachers opened my mind to many ideas—including possibilities. I remember reading the little blue biography books in elementary school. I particularly liked reading about Thomas Alva Edison. He reflected, "Just because something doesn't do what you planned it to do doesn't mean it's useless." I was taught to learn from failure as well as success. I was taught to persevere—that failure was only a temporary condition and that dreams coupled with hard work could come true. We teachers must teach reality. The world is not always "warm and fuzzy" and "feel good" in its offerings to us. But the real world has endless possibilities for all of us if we dedicate ourselves to working toward those possibilities. We teachers must teach flexibility and the opportunities that change brings with it.

One more thing comes to mind that my teachers—all of them from elementary through high school—did for me. THEY MADE ME READ. They made me into a voracious reader who devoured all genres of the printed word. We teachers need to create readers, real readers, not "scrolling down" readers.

I hope some food for thought has been spread out for figurative consumption and intellectual digestion in this rather informal essay. I confess that I do not know all the answers as to how to teach our students to lead literate lives. I merely offer some knowledge gained from experience teaching and observation of life. I must defer to Oscar Wilde and agree with him when he said, "I am not young enough to know everything."

Smitty

I was not impressed the first time I met him in Natchez, Mississippi, in June 1949. He was a poorly-educated junior high school dropout, a simple country boy not yet thirty years old with very little money. His future did not seem especially promising because of his disability. Most other people were not impressed when they first met him either, and probably all of them were not aware of his disability. He hid that well. I did not even realize it at that initial meeting. But I did not know much or realize much or recognize much of anything when I first met him. I was only a few minutes old there in the Natchez General Hospital. This man was my father.

As I grew up, I learned more about this simple man. I knew that he went to work every day and sometimes at night. I knew his disability. In World War II, he had been severely wounded, which resulted in his right leg being amputated just below the knee and a couple of fingers on one hand being amputated as well. He always strapped on an artificial leg of wood and metal. The only time I ever heard him complain was about the irritation on the stump of his leg from the rubbing of the artificial leg that he wore. It was probably before I was ten years old that I asked him what did he think when they told him that they would have to cut off his leg. He replied, "What would you think?" He did not have to say anything more.

As I grew older, I learned more about the life of my father—but not all from him. He did not discuss his life very much. He sidestepped questions. He had three older sisters who told my younger sisters and me bits and pieces of the story of his life, mostly after he died. He was orphaned as a baby and put in a Jackson, Mississippi, orphanage with one of his sisters. His mother had died of malnutrition while holding him, a few-days-old infant, in her arms. A family adopted him. His adopted family did not maintain ties with him after he left to join the military in July 1940. He kept one picture of his adoptive mother. We went to the funeral of his adoptive mother when I was a senior in high school. That was the only and last connection with his adopting family that I know. Something must have carried him through these trying times in his life.

As I have said, he went to work at some kind of job almost every day of his life. Because of his lack of education as well as his disability, he worked at a variety of low-paying jobs. The government had awarded him a compensation for his war wounds, but he was not 100% pensioned. The compensation dollars were helpful but not sustaining for a family. He continued to work. As I grew up and attended school, he always advised me to get my education—as much as possible—because, according to him, once that education was in my head, no one could take that away from me. He said that education was the way out of poverty.

As for his time in the service in World War II, he rarely talked with his family about it. He downplayed his injuries. I knew that he had served with the First Cavalry Division. I knew he was a machine gunner. I knew from a uniform shirt he had kept that he was a staff sergeant when discharged. I remember seeing a couple of pictures of him wearing it. I remember only one story about the war he told. It was about one Japanese soldier surrendering to Americans. He had his hands up a bit when he first appeared to surrender; and then when he walked in among the American soldiers, he raised his hands and arms high, triggering hand grenades he had hidden on himself in his clothes. The Japanese soldier died, along with several GIs. I remember, too, that he showed me the Purple Heart awarded to him. He mentioned he had some battle and campaign ribbons. I saw his Combat Infantryman Badge. I remember seeing a Bronze Star he had been awarded.

He served in the Asiatic-Pacific Theater in New Guinea, the Bismarck Archipelago, the Southern Philippines, and the Northern Philippines. He was wounded at Luzon in the Philippine Islands in early March, 1945. He was honorably discharged from Lawson General Hospital in Atlanta, Georgia, in late April, 1946. He never talked about what he went through during this 14-month period. That time must have been a personal hell, added to the general hell of the jungle war in the Pacific. I can only imagine the sheer physical pain, the inner mental anguish of an amputation, the suffering through rehabilitation, the phantom limb issues, and the agony of social adjustment. Something inside him must have carried him through this time serving his country in the military.

I remember both of my parents telling me that early in their marriage they had a nice house in a nice neighborhood in Natchez. But the house was destroyed in a fire, and from that point on, their life swooped downward into a constant "rob Peter to pay Paul" household economics. Through it all, my father continued to work to pay the bills. Nothing seemed to make life easier for him. Nothing in his life in these times existed that would impress anyone it seemed.

Then in 1980, mother had exploratory surgery. It was pancreatic cancer. That news hit all of us very hard—especially my father, who had been married to her for over 35 years! I remember he broke down once in my presence; he shed tears and questioned me, "What am I going to do without your mama?" She literally withered away in front of us for eleven months. Something inside him must have carried him through the everyday money and life struggles.

My father died of a heart attack in 1988. Many people told me after his funeral that they did not know he was an amputee and had an artificial leg. I replied that unless a person knew about his disability, most people did not even notice the slight gimp in his walk and that he did not talk much about it. Looking through old papers and other items from the attic, I recently looked at his discharge papers. I remembered the places listed where he served; I remembered the Purple Heart; but I did not remember his being awarded four Bronze Stars.

Now my life span has exceeded that of my father, I look at his military record summation and think that he never told me or my sisters much about his military service. Thinking back over his life, I have decided that this man, James Thomas Smith, has impressed me with his optimistic American spirit that carried him through World War II service and the remainder of his life as a disabled American veteran.

Antiquarian Angst

"Ozymandias," the lesson's focus
Change, the central locus
Teacher wish for hocus pocus
Student attitude quite atrocious

Teacher wrinkled lip with frown
No more on a pedestal looking 'round
A shattered visage, feeling down
Gone is the old learning ground

Students with electronics in hand
Chrome book and tablet mock where I stand
On the boundless and level sand
I am the "traveler" from the antique land.

The Best Decision I Ever Made

I remember a time when I was younger than ten that my mother and I walked a couple of miles to a store in the little town in which we lived. My father had driven the only car we had to work in a nearby city. Being a little boy, I really did not know how poor in the socio-economic sense we were at the time. On the way home, quite heavy rain began to fall on us as we walked. We had nowhere to go to get out of the rain except for the open garage next to a house. We stood huddled together at the very edge under the garage's sheltering roof. I could hear the people inside the house. I was nervous and afraid that we would be discovered by the people who were inside the house. What would they say to us? What would they do to us? Would they summon the police? I felt embarrassment and shame as we stood there for a few minutes as the rain continued and then stopped. The time had dragged by as I stood by my mother. I did not like the situation we were in. I was so relieved when I felt my mother's gentle but strong hand on my shoulder. My mother ushered me out as the rain let up. She was stoically silent. We walked to our home. This memory is forever etched in my mind.

As a young boy, I did not like the situation we were in that day. I did not realize it then, but that situation my mother and I were in at that time probably shaped my future more than any other single event in my early life. It was most probably the best decision I ever made—even though at the time, I did not know I made a decision at a subconscious level. I made the subconscious decision to always do my best in school in order to rise out of poverty.

Yes, we were poor. We lived in a little house on the other side of the large earthen levee surrounding and protecting the small town in central Louisiana. The house was built by my father and uncle. Initially it was very small with one large room. In two or three years the house was doubled in size with the new section divided into two rooms. The house was not insulated, nor was there any source of heat other than a wood-burning stove at one end of the older section of the house. No indoor plumbing existed within the house. The bare wood of the outer walls and the 2x4s showed on the inside of the rooms. Several years later my father and uncle would put sheet rock on the walls and build a small bathroom with only cold water onto the back of the house. About the same time they put in a butane heater in the front room and in the bathroom. The house had fans to circulate the hot air during the long, hot Louisiana summers and had a second-hand air conditioner for the front room of the house for a year or so before I graduated from high school. But that house was my home.

Yes, we were poor in material things but not in love and family. I have fond memories of events and family in that house we called home. My mother had graduated from high school in that small town when the school had only eleven grades. I do not know if her brothers and sister completed high school or not. My father had dropped out of school in the junior high years and eventually joined the army before World War II. He served in the Pacific Theater and almost died from wounds suffered in the Philippines. He lost one leg just below the knee and parts of several of his fingers on one hand. He was the victim of informal discrimination against the disabled the remainder of his life. He received a small government compensation; jobs that he had paid little. I remember my mother sitting at the kitchen table with paper and pencil, trying to "figure out" which bills to pay when and with what little money our household had at any given time. But my loving parents made that house a home for my two sisters and me.

My parents inculcated in me a desire to get an education to make my life better than the life that they had. That process had begun before the time my mother and I stepped out of the rain to just inside the garage that belonged to someone else. That time I felt nervous, afraid, embarrassed, and ashamed. It was that time I thought I never wanted to be in that situation again. It was that time that I subconsciously made the best decision that I ever made—to complete my education to better myself for the future. That decision has paid dividends to the present. I am a teacher. I do not have excessive money, but I am much better off than my parents who had rather hard lives. My wife and I are comfortable financially and do not owe anyone. But there are other dividends yielded by an education, including helping others succeed, working with good people, inspiring and being inspired by students and colleagues, and contributing to the future of our nation and its citizens. That subconscious decision morphed itself into a more concrete, conscious on-going decision as I grew older.

Somehow I believe that my decision was guided by the real hand of my mother on my shoulder on that rainy day and the figurative hand of my mother on my shoulder the rest of my life. That rainy-day memory is forever with me. The decision stays with me as well.

The American Spirit: An American History Confidential

I am American history. I inform all people of many things—one of which is the American spirit. Some people insist that the American spirit is arrogant and that it promotes American exceptionalism because it assumed the named "America" just for the United States of America and because it has "star-spangled" eyes. But historical perspective is everything. I know. Do not judge American history or the American spirit with a chronocentric view. Do not judge without truly knowing each. One had to be there, to live there, to experience the times, to be a denizen of the times. However, through good times and bad times the American spirit always existed—sometimes it flourished, and sometimes it was less viable.

The "American spirit" is an intangible that can be seen, felt, sensed, aroused, provoked, and otherwise manifested, employed, wielded, utilized, exerted, directed, believed in, appreciated, demonstrated, and more. This indefinable, elusive term "American spirit" birthed itself even before the United States of America itself emerged from the British colonies along the Atlantic coast of North America. Its collective fathers and mothers were those men and women in the Old World who dreamed of a new life and new opportunities in the New World. These new opportunities manifested themselves the most in what became the United States of America. The opportunities proved not to be tasks easily accomplished and not always pleasant. But an element of the spirit is an indefatigable energy.

Let me remind you of a few people, locations, and events that illustrated, forged, and invigorated the American spirit. Remember the explorers setting foot in the New World, the starving time in early Jamestown, the Pilgrims and their Mayflower Compact, the Boston Tea Party, the fiery voice of Patrick Henry, the plain words of Thomas Paine, the beautiful, profound words of the Declaration of Independence, Valley Forge, and the Constitutional Convention? Recall the Tripolitan War, the "rockets' red glare" on Fort McHenry, the stirring words of *The Liberator*, the rallying cries of the Texans in their war for independence, the Trail of Tears, the Spot Resolutions of the Mexican War, the Seneca Falls Convention, the immigrant masses, "California or Bust" on the canvas covering of a Conestoga wagon, and Bleeding Kansas? Recollect the Lincoln-Douglas Debates, the Emancipation Proclamation, Sharpsburg, Gettysburg, Sherman's comment on war, Lee's Farewell to his Army of Northern Virginia, and Reconstruction? I continue and ask you to bring to mind Wounded Knee, Bryan's "Cross of Gold" speech, the Rough Riders, the Doughboys in World War I, what FDR said we had to fear, that "day of infamy," the GIs in World War II liberating Europe and Asia, the Marshall Plan, the Berlin Airlift, *Brown v. Board of Education*, and the Peace Corps. Think back about the Vietnam War—the soldiers and the protesters, Martin Luther King, Jr., and the Civil Rights Movement, Americans on the moon, Gerald Ford saying "the long national nightmare is over," a President saying, "Mr. Gorbachev, tear down this wall!," September 11, and computers and the Internet. The American spirit was in all of these!

But the American spirit had, perhaps, greater presence in not-so-famous people. I, American history, have witnessed more private and personal examples of the American spirit. I felt it in the helping hand extended to a neighbor in the early colonies. I sensed it in the hearts and minds of the yeoman farmer and his wife when they realized their dream of owning their own farm in frontier America. The merchant who boycotted British goods aroused the spirit in his customers as he stood up against the might of the British Empire. The British, ordering the rebels to disperse, provoked it in the minutemen on the village green of Lexington. It manifested itself in the courage of the sailors who heard John Paul Jones' yell to the British, "I have not yet begun to fight!" This spirit is employed by the little girl who opens her own lemonade stand in the summer. The spirit is wielded by the school kids who raised money for a disabled veteran's new home. Ordinary citizens utilize the American spirit in team effort to carry out a project. That spirit exerts itself in the pride of workmanship of the typical American laborer. It is directed by the opportunities available to Americans who will work to better themselves. The American spirit is believed in by the young man born in poverty who now has a college degree and is on his way up the socio-economic ladder. It is appreciated by the mother of a malnourished baby in Africa when she is handed a CARE package from the USA. The veteran confined in the wheel chair demonstrated the American spirit as he struggles to stand and salute the American flag passing by in a parade. The American spirit is exhibited in overseas relief efforts, international rescue missions, space exploration, generous aid to help with natural disasters, and willingness to get involved.

I am American history. James Baldwin summed me up as follows: "American history is longer, larger, more various, more beautiful, and more terrible than anything anyone has ever said about it." I acknowledge some terrible times inherent in my timeline, but the American spirit has overarching goodness and energy and benevolence. But I wish to paraphrase Baldwin by saying, "American spirit is more enduring, greater, more various, more beautiful, and more embracing than anything anyone has ever said about it."

Now I ask you what represents the American spirit more than anything else? What one symbol embodies the American spirit more so than anything else? That symbol is the flag of the United States of America—the Stars and Stripes, Old Glory. That flag is all around. I see a flag carried by a color guard in a parade. I see a flag on postage stamps. I see flags on flagpoles outside schools and businesses. I see a small flag on a desk in a home office. I see a flag attached to a wall in a family room. I see a flag that covered a casket briefly now folded carefully and displayed in a triangular case on a shelf in a home. But remember what Anthony Liccione stated about the flag: "The American flag doesn't give her glory on a peaceful, calm day. It's when the winds pick up and become boisterous, do we see her strength." That time, too, is when everyone sees the strength of the American spirit. And that is the very time the vitality and fervor of the American spirit is needed in the world, and that is the time it always ascends.

Perhaps, when it comes to the average American as well as the not-so-average American, something that was said by Robert F. Kennedy brings that spirit into sharp acuity: "There are those that look at things the way they are, and ask why? I dream of things that never were, and ask why not?"

The American spirit endures, and I, American history, am its chronicler.

Street Preacher

I listened as I walked.
I heard him as he talked.
I saw him draw a crowd.
I heard him very loud.

He, to make his point, screamed.
He asked if we had dreamed.
He spoke, "Believe in Christ!"
He spat, "Evil enticed!"

They mostly kept walking.
They really were balking.
They think he is surreal.
They ignore his loud appeal.

We are the same I thought.
We paid attention naught.
We did not heed this man.
We do not need His plan.

They pass, turning each head.
They look away instead.
They, too busy to stop.
They think, "Where is the cop?"

He, a wilderness voice.
He says we have a choice.
He calls out "Salvation!"
He quotes Revelation.

I, taken back, did halt.
I judge "It's not my fault?"
I think his speech purloins.
I did toss him some coins.

Statement of Pedagogy and Beliefs

I am rather eclectic in my pedagogical approaches to teaching. I will use whatever approach—whether it be pedagogical or andragogical—with a class depending on the student makeup of the class, the time frame of the class, and the particular subject matter of the day. I do not believe that there is only one way to teach.

I am a humanist in many of my ideas about teaching. Decisions should be made with the learner in mind. Whatever yields the greatest benefit for students should be the dominant factor in the decision-making process.

Several years ago, I became aware of an essay entitled "Finding Connie in the Rock." In the essay, history and political science professor Joe Dunn describes his personal teaching style and his methods like that of Michelangelo freeing David he envisioned in the sculptor's stone. Dunn hopes to "free Connie for successful learning." He concludes that "as teachers we are all sculptors" and that we should "keep envisioning, chiseling, and shaping." We should challenge students with high expectations. Colleagues and friends describe Dunn as a good example of the "sage on the stage" who uses provocative teaching techniques of a high-energy expert that inspires students to do their best.

Thomas McDaniel, a colleague of Dunn's, wrote a response to the essay in which he says that Dunn's style is not the only effective or good way to teach. Other professors emphasize hands-on approaches, stress collaborative learning, etc. Building on strengths as well as eliminating weaknesses of students are both good teaching means. McDaniel goes on to say that no single teaching style has a monopoly on pedagogical impact and that we would do well to honor the diversity of teaching styles that abound in higher education. I agree with Dunn and McDaniel.

As I stated previously, I do not believe that there is only one way to teach. I primarily use the lecture/discussion method in college courses. But I do use critical questions for writing, role-playing simulations, student group work, student presentations, etc., when I think they are appropriate ways to maximize student learning. All methods were successful because teaching styles were matched with learning styles when it came to the nature of the subject matter.

I see much value in Knowles' andragogical theory and Bruner's constructivist theory—even when applied to traditional students. I believe in building upon or connecting to what students already know. Bridging to prior knowledge works.

I realize that there is and has been for a time a paradigm shift in higher education from teacher-focus to student-focus learning because of the changing student population demographics in post-secondary education. We teachers must be aware of that transition in focus of the teaching-learning process.

We teachers must be aware, too, of the fact that even though we love our discipline, most of our students do not love our favorite subject. We teachers must work to show the importance of our discipline and its practical applications in today's world. When we can instill in students the value of our particular subject matter, the students will embrace it more fully and learn more.

I tell my students that they must know facts, concepts, and perspectives for me as their teacher. I try to show how the past has fashioned all of us into what we are today. I try to equip students to understand their own collective past and themselves in order to understand other people in this diversely populated world.

Returning to the analogy of finding Connie in the rock, I would say that it may not be in our best interests to think of students as products, nor even as works of art to be shaped and polished by the teacher-as-sculptor. But the analogy validates my convictions that teaching is a science with theories and applications and other professional pedagogy but also that teaching is an art with vision and craftsmanship and human passion.

Midnight Motor Parts—Radio Spot

(Introduction—sound of tires squealing out with "Little GTO," "Mustang Sally," or other car songs)

Announcer: Listen out there all you car freaks, car owners, car drivers, truck owners, truck drivers, RV livers, pimp-my-riders, gearheads, daddies of teen-age drivers, little old ladies from Pasadena, and everybody else who's ever seen a car, truck, or van. Have you ever needed a part for your vehicle and could not get it for a week or more from Mr. Goodwrench, your local mechanic, auto parts store, the dealership where you bought your hotrod, or your brother-in-law Percival? Boy, were you ever hacked! You had to bum a ride with the jerk down the street, stand and wait for the bus, stand and wait for the subway to stand to travel to work, carpool with the boss and his nephews, or walk and hitch. And then you had to call daily to hassle the service department manager, so he wouldn't forget you. Well, that's some bummer! You don't deserve that kind of treatment. You need us, Midnight Motor Parts. We don't have Mr. Goodwrench; we have Mr. Fastwrench. We guarantee your needed parts in your hands in less than 24 hours. We deliver. We really deliver because our stores are mobile. Yes, the whole store comes to you! We actually deliver.

And you save money because we don't have low overhead; we have no overhead. You can't find us in the yellow pages. You can find us on your local street corner. Watch for our company vans and friendly personnel. They're the ones who say, "Hey, Mac!"

Our mobile Midnight Motor Parts vans are everywhere. So is our stock of quality previously-owned automotive parts. Whatever you need, come to us. Don't go to a one-location salvage yard or a nationwide chain store. Remember we deliver. We deliver from our vast storehouse of parts. Our units with Mr. Fastwrenches comb the neighborhood streets near you for your needed part for fast delivery. If the part is not available locally, we check parking buildings and garages all over the city. Once your make and model vehicle is spotted, Mr. Fastwrench works quickly to procure your part. Then we hurry to deliver to you.

Our prices are unbelievable. We have slashed everything, including some police car tires. Our technicians are the best money can bail out of jail. Our drivers really move their tail lights for you. Our distributors offer you less-than-wholesale prices and tested, working products. Midnight Motor Parts. We deliver. Remember our guarantee: If we can't get your needed part, we'll get you a car. Guaranteed. Midnight Motor Parts. We're on your corner. Watch for us. Sorry no credit or debit cards accepted. No checks either. Cash only. You understand.

(Sound of tires squealing out.)

A Message from Your Grandfather

Hello, little one. This is your grandfather writing to you before you are born. You really have two grandfathers, but your other grandfather on your mother's side is already in heaven. So I will have to be rather like two-grandfathers-in-one for you. I shall do my best. You do not know me yet, but you will. I am sure of that. I do not know if you are a boy or a girl. It really does not matter. I just want you to be born healthy and your beautiful mother to be healthy, too.

When your Grandmother Sue and I received the news that you were to be born into your mom and dad's household, we were ecstatic! Your dad told us by phone, and we literally danced with joy! We are so happy that soon you will be with us! We pray for you and your mother several times daily. We want you to arrive in this world happy and healthy.

I want you to know how special you are. You are already loved by so many people! You have many, many fine relatives on both sides of your family. You will have many wonderful friends. You have marvelous, loving parents. You could not ask for a better Mom and Dad. They will be devoted to you. Always love and respect them.

You are an important person already. I want you to know that you will have opportunities to grow and develop your individual personality and talents. I know that you will grow up to be an exceptional adult. You have potential; I advise you to develop what talents God gives you. You may become an astronaut, an electrical engineer, a writer, a research chemist, a teacher, or any of a myriad of other professions or occupations. I want you to be a caring and compassionate person. Even though you are little and do not understand my words at the moment, I offer them to you with love and affection. I hope your mom and dad will read this message to you several times before you are born and keep it for you for when you are older. I hope that you read it often as you grow up.

I anticipate your birth in late summer with great joy. I will retire from my first career in education a short while before you are born. Your Grandmother Sue and I will move to Michigan to live close to you and your mom and dad. When you need to get away from Mom and Dad for a while, our house will be open for you to visit. You will have to allow your Grandmother Sue to spoil you just a bit. Is that OK with you? We can talk about that subject more at a later time when you can talk or, at least, smile. If you smile at your Grandmother Sue, you can get your way much of the time. Just keep that bit of advice in the back of your mind for now. It will work on your redheaded Aunt Paige, too. Try it out!

Oh, yes, I will want you to go to Disney World with me some time in the future. That Mickey Mouse just has to meet you! We will check him out together one day soon. I know we will have to take your Grandmother Sue with us. Your mom and dad will probably go, too; but we won't make them if they have to work!

God loves you, little one. Your Grandmother Sue and I love you, too. We wish you the best in your life. We pray that you have a long, happy, healthy, successful Christian life serving your fellow man and woman and God Almighty. May God bless you and your parents. May God guide you and keep you and may His Grace shine from within you.

I give you this last humble advice. Love God. Love your nation. Love your parents. Respect yourself and others. Work hard. Develop the potential you have. Serve others. Be a "giver" and not a "taker." As Johann W. von Goethe, a famous German philosopher, said, "Treat people as if they were what they ought to be and you will help them to become what they are capable of being." Remember God's Golden Rule and practice it.

Here are "Twelve Principles of Success" compiled from Frederick Douglass' life and writings.

- Understanding that the proper use of power is to help others.
- Giving up something you want in order to help someone else.
- Learning how to challenge and overcome doubt.

- Understanding why and how to control the human ego.
- Doing what is right and proper without delay, even if no one is looking.
- Learning how to use knowledge and understanding wisely.
- Overcoming indecisiveness by developing proper organizational skills.
- Making gratitude a part of every thought and action.
- Practicing the skill of listening before making judgments.
- Remaining true to your word.
- Practicing the art of giving without expecting something in return.
- Recognizing that success is as much a motivation to others as to you.

Apply these principles to your life, and you will do well.

    I will keep you in my heart and mind as long as I live. You are already a part of me. You shall always be.

Your Grandfather Smith

February 21, 2004

An Address Given at the Roast of Retiring Principal Julius Guillot

May 1986

With Apologies—Not Really—to Red Buttons

The question tonight is why are we giving this man a dinner? Think of all the famous individuals that never got a dinner!

Alexander Hamilton, the financial wizard of the young United States, who put this country on a sound financial basis by issuing ten dollar bills with his picture on them, never got a dinner!

Nathan Hale, the American patriot during the Revolutionary War, who made a name for himself as a spy who happened to be hanging around in British territory to secure information for our side, never got a dinner! He got a necktie party that he was all choked up about, but he never got a dinner!

Count Dracula, the famous Transylvanian nobleman, who operated a blood bank in his basement, never got a dinner. He had been invited to several banquets, but he never got past the first bite. Anyway, I hear they saved a stake for him. But he never got a dinner!

Clara Peller, the grand old lady of Wendy's TV commercials, never got a dinner! Why do you think she's always saying, "Where's the beef?" The old lady is hungry because she never got a dinner!

Moses, the great Old Testament figure, never got a dinner. Moses led his people out of bondage in Egypt. He even parted the Red Sea with his bare hands! Did he ever get a dinner? No! All he ever got was a headache from the hot desert sun and two tablets. He never got a dinner!

Mary, Queen of Scots, never got a dinner. No one even "axed" her! Oops! On second thought she was "axed"! But she never got a dinner!

Joan of Arc, leader of the French against the English oppressors in France, never got a dinner! She rallied the French people to drive out the English overlords. She never got a dinner! She was at a barbecue given in her honor! But she never got a dinner!

Why are we giving this man a dinner? What did he ever do? This question bothered me, so I did some research. Guillot. The name Guillot. I checked the encyclopedia. Do you know what I found? The closest entry to Guillot was g-u-i-l-l-o-t-i-n-e. Guillotine! That's right! This man invented the guillotine! You don't believe me? Just ask some teachers who say that they have had their heads chopped off! Maybe that's why we're giving him a dinner!

Think about it! He's come to school for years. We never gave him a dinner. But when he says he's not coming back, we give him a dinner!

I suppose it's just our way of saying, "We'll miss you."

Christmas in My Heart

Tucked in with the movie gift card, the little slip of paper had these words and letters written on it: "Mom—IOU one Christmas Disney Photo Calendar—TS." It is Christmas 2015.

Our son Tom, his beautiful wife Sarah, and their two young sons J.T. and Christopher thus continued to give my wife Sue the best Christmas gift she ever received each Christmas. The giving of this best Christmas gift ever first occurred in 2010 when Tom handed his mother a wrapped gift that was thin like a paper tablet. In that year all of us had visited Disney World as a family, and Sue and I had arranged and paid for my two sisters to be there as well. My mother had always said she and our father wanted to take us to Disneyland when we were young children, but the money was never there for such a trip.

Sue unwrapped her gift that was a Disney calendar. She saw that it was personalized with monthly pictures of all of us there for the family gathering. Tears welled up in her eyes, and she openly cried with tears of joy. As we flipped the month pages, we saw heartfelt memories that will last for a lifetime. This family picture calendar was, indeed, the best Christmas gift ever for Sue. Her tears of happiness marked it in my memory.

But I have another Christmas gift memory marked by tears of joy by another mom. That "mom" was my mother. It was December, 1967. I was a freshman at Northeast Louisiana State College and had a weekend/holiday job at a lock and dam construction site. That job provided me some money to buy special Christmas presents for the first time because otherwise we were quite poor. As always, money was scarce at my house. Daddy, a disabled veteran, worked at whatever low-paying jobs he could get. Because Mama always paid bills and took care of family as well as she could, she neglected herself when it came to most every situation. She sacrificed for others. This Christmas, because I had a little money, I wanted to get something special for Mama. My girlfriend Sue and I thought about and hunted for the perfect gift for

Mama to no avail until I remembered that her wedding ring had worn through and that she had placed it several months ago in a jewelry store in Natchez, Mississippi, for repair. That ring, because of her generosity to others, remained in the repair shop in that jewelry store and not on her finger and probably would remain there for quite a time. I told Sue that we would pay for the repair and get her wedding ring back to her for Christmas. That would be the perfect gift I knew because of the sentimental attachment!

Sue and I traveled to Natchez and went to the store to inquire about the beloved ring. While waiting for the clerk going in the back to seek the ring, I had thoughts of the ring being misplaced or lost. After an anxious wait, he returned to us, carrying Mama's ring. The clerk carefully put the repaired ring in a small box and put it in a small brown paper bag.

Christmas was only a couple of days away, but we could not wait to give Mama her perfect Christmas present. At the kitchen table the three of us sat. We told Mama we had something for her, and she smiled warmly at both of us as only a mother can do. She probably knew that within eight months Sue and I would be married. I placed the small folded bag from my pocket on the table before her. She continued to smile but looked quizzically at the bag as she reached for it. She pulled out the small box, and her smile evaporated from her face. Her hands trembled a bit as she removed the top. Her eyes brightened and glistened with tears that streamed down her face. Her face beamed as another smile formed there. She nodded at us and slipped the ring onto its rightful place on her finger. She was speechless but held her arms out to us. We both embraced her as she continued to weep tears of joy and then whispered, "Thank you." I felt her warm tears on my cheek. She smiled a genuine Christmas smile. I knew this was the best Christmas present that I would ever give.

I did not think much about this repaired ring Christmas gift until over ten years later. It was Monday before Thanksgiving in 1980. The Christmas season was upon us once more. But this time there was little happiness. Mama had fought cancer for ten months and was in the final stages. We had spent the weekend with Mama and Daddy and had packed the car to go home for a few days until Thanksgiving when we would return. We had hugged goodbye in the small room where Mama sat. I was last to leave and turned at the door to look at her again. She smiled the Christmas smile at me as she had done years ago when Sue and I had given her back her wedding ring. Her eyes brightened for a few minutes. I went back over to her, hugged her again, and held her hand in mine briefly. "I love you, Mother," I said. Her weak hand grasped mine tightly for a brief moment, and I felt her wedding ring press into my fingers. That special Christmas from years ago came back into my mind. Mama died one week later.

    That year we celebrated Christmas without Mama. But I always remember Christmas 1967 because of the perfect gift I gave. Now each Christmas that our son, his wife, and sons give my wife Sue a Christmas calendar because it is a perfect gift for her, that act of love stirs in me the 1967 Christmas when I, too, gave the perfect Christmas gift. But now as I grow older, I realize that when I gave that best gift I ever gave, I actually received the best gift ever given because I now have that special Christmas memory of my mother every year; and it is renewed by my son's best Christmas gift ever to his mother each Christmas. That special calendar ensures that all year long I have Christmas in my heart.

Star-Spangled Eyes

I, with my family, stood on the international bridge
>over the Rio Grande,
Looking into Mexico.

Below me, on the near bank was another
>man with his family,
Looking into the United States.

Through a hole in the fence, he carefully handed his small child
>to his wife.

"Illegal aliens," I told my family as I pointed, "coming to
>America."

That sight is forever burned into my memory.
>It haunts.

What I took for granted, he pursues.

That father had star-spangled eyes, and he gave

>me back mine.

("Star-Spangled Eyes" was first published int the Spring 2001 issue of *Trends and Issues: The Quarterly Publication of the Florida Council for the Social Studies*.)

He ART To Be in Pictures

"And past the cast of
a thousand stares. He awoke
to find a beckoning call."

Gabriel George Bell found his beckoning call—the life of a professional artist. The above lines of poetry are his. The beckoning call is his, too. "I must paint this weekend," he said after a week in training and general preparation in his new job as a state correctional officer at Angola, the Louisiana State Penitentiary. Gabriel took this job in order to be able to afford to buy paint and quality materials for his work as an artist and not to have to worry about paying the rent. He says being a painter is like being a runner. A runner who stops running for a few days loses something. He, as a painter, loses something, too, if he doesn't paint daily.

Gabriel Bell was born in Alexandria, Louisiana, in 1952. He attended school there and graduated from Menard in 1970. Father Richard Fale was his art teacher at Menard. After high school, Gabriel attended LSU-A for two years as a fine arts major in education. Drafted in 1972, Gabriel served in Italy. While there, he basked in the art of Vatican City, Rome, Pisa, and Milan. After the military, he completed an art school correspondence course.

As a resident of Alexandria, Gabriel had opportunities to display his works. Among them were a one-man show at LSU-A and exhibitions at Addler's of New Orleans, the Collector's Gallery in Baton Rouge, and the Courtney Gallery of Art in Alexandria. As an Alexandrian, Gabriel painted a "landmark series" of the city and gained recognition for the city and himself.

Now Gabriel Bell lives in a little yellow house on Bordelon Street in the shadow of the water tower in Hessmer, Louisiana, in Avoyelles Parish. The artist in him wanted a change. Gabriel wants to be a regionalist. He desires to paint a particular type of people, a particular uniqueness of a region. Acadiana and its rich French culture is that region. Avoyelles Parish is his starting point.

Gabriel has done several works already. Two come to mind. His *Man from Avoyelles*, a portrait of his friend Keith Chatelain, shows a Frenchman wearing his favorite shirt, sitting on a couch covered with his grandmother's quilt. Gabriel wants a person looking at the portrait *Man from Avoyelles* to be able to say, "That looks like a Frenchman from Louisiana." The painting, according to Gabriel, denotes a simplistic life, which is important to Gabriel as a person. This dry-brush painting was the first time in years that he spent two months working on one painting. The other work that is prominent is the painting of a small chicken coop that is in the backyard of Keith Chatelain's parents' place near Mansura. This chicken coop is the last live stop for chickens. Their next stop is the dinner table. The work is titled *Death Row*. Ironically, Gabriel's first stop in his new job at Angola was death row.

Gabriel Bell has said his style is inspired by Andrew Wyeth. Once in 1975 Gabriel telephoned Wyeth, who lived in Pennsylvania. The well-known artist and the lesser-known artist politely discussed the climate in the respective states.

Gabriel looks at his works and does not want to "rest on his laurels." He does not really like to hold onto his works. If he keeps a favorite work for too long, he says he can get delusions of grandeur and becomes too attached to it and then overprices it.

But Gabriel insists that he must become emotionally attached to his subjects, whether they be persons or places. He must "know" the person or place to do what he deems a good job.

He states matter-of-factly that he is not a portrait painter, but a landscape painter. In either case, however, Gabriel wants to be invisible as an artist in relation to his subject. He wants to capture the natural setting or the natural person with his brush and paints.

Inspiration is all he needs to paint. He has no problem with technique or materials or location. He's painted in the kitchen, in the living room, in the backyard, in the back of a pickup truck, and in a field. His painting skills are portable.

In a June 13, 1976, article in the *Alexandria Daily Town Talk*, Gabriel Bell stated, "I have a drive . . . a creativity within me . . . that not everyone has. It's as though God were pushing me to paint. That is why I paint. I like to find the 'soul' or worth in even the most ordinary and even ugly things I see."

Gabriel Bell is constantly looking for a spark what will ignite his imagination. He observes the world around him and thinks in planar values, in light and dark shades, in textures, and in colors. A painting appears in his creative mind and then is transformed by his talent into a work of art, a picture from his mind's eye.

Gabe Bell once described himself in a letter as a "good old boy." He is one of us. He is just folks. But he is more, too. He is an artist. Lines of his poem relate undeniably to himself and his work.

> "He walks and talks
> to self the same and asks
> of self to please remain."

(This article/essay about Gabe Bell, now a noted artist, was written in the late 1980s. The last I heard about him was an article in a newspaper highlighting his work on murals at the central Louisiana veteran's medical complex. I have one painting of an Alexandria, Louisiana, building that he gave me and several pictures of his artwork from the time of the article/essay. His work is impressive.)

Huey Dewey Lewis and the Bad News Retro Concert—A Radio Spot

(Huey Lewis and the News music introduction and background)

Casey Kasem-like Voice: Hey, all you baby boomers out there! Are you tired of your teen-ager having his music blaring too loud throughout your home, even though he's using earphones? Do you have weak eardrums from your teen-age daughter's boyfriends blasting the atmosphere on your side of the planet Earth when they drive down your street and into your driveway? Are you fed up with obscene, mean, and unclean videoes? Are you tired of your teen-ager begging for and spending all your extra cash for his kind of rock-and-roll music, of rock-and-roll rap, of rock-and-roll retardedness? Have you fussed and fussed but to no avail?

Well, here's what you do. Here's your ticket to peace and quiet, to sanity, to sweet revenge! Yes, ticket, or rather tickets. You can send your teen-agers to a rock-and-roll concert of your own choosing. Buy tickets for them to Huey Dewey Lewis and the Bad News Concert and require they attend this 48-hour lock-in concert. Doors will absolutely be locked down at 8 p. m. Friday evening, and time locks will be applied to all doors of the stadium. Uniformed police will be on duty around the clock. Don't worry—those teen-agers won't be able to get out until 8 p. m. Sunday! You can have control of the music at your home and in your neighborhood.

But listen to what your teen-agers will be experiencing at the concert. First, all cell phones are confiscated. Of course, they will hear the hits of Huey Dewey Lewis and the Bad News. But there are many other artists and groups that will perform live! For this concert, many big names will be there. Contractual and time-sharing agreements have resulted in several artists and groups' merging their talents. So old and new and young and old will combine talents for your teen-ager's listening agony and ecstasy. Here are some of the performing artists and groups scheduled to appear: George Michaels Jackson, Flood the Church,

Beastie Bellamy Brother Boys, the Righteous Doobie Brothers, Joe Jackson Browne, Sly and the Family Bad Company, and Cheap Humble Pie Trick.

Sounds good for those teen-agers in your life? But you say they'll balk at going because of the contractual combining of groups? Teen-agers won't even notice. They don't listen to anything you say, anyway. They'll just pick up on some old hot rock-and-roll names and jump at the chance to get concert tickets and tour T-shirts. Remember how stupid you were between 13 and 19 years old?

Here are a few more performers who'll be there: Tom Petty and the Traveling U2s, New Loverboys on the Block, Ratt Poison, 2-Live Jive Bunny Crew, Miami Sound Master Mixers, 10,000 Technotronics, and Killer Dwarfs and the Good Girls.

You're thinking this is the concert of the year to send you teen-ager off to, aren't you? We knew it. You deserve a break, and so do we! Tickets are only $39.95 each. So, call the station now to get details to reserve your teen-ager's place in the stadium and your peace of mind for 48 hours. At the door will be standing room only, and prices will be slightly higher—only $139.78. Tickets are also available at the usual Ticketmaster Outlets and your local high school principal's office. Don't wait until there are no tickets left and get bad news! Get your Bad News tickets now! Sorry, President and Mrs. Obama will not be in attendance. This is an Exile Productions Company, Ltd., concert and meets all FDA nutritional standards, plus it's caffeine free—except at the concession stands! Get your teen-ager in the concert and out of your hair. Your teen-ager will never be the same. They'll be afraid you'll send them to our next scheduled concert—the Grateful Rolling Dead Stones with a very old Mick Jagger!

Letter to Coach of the New Orleans Saints

November 15, 2009

Coach Payton,

I am a Saints' fan of long-standing from 1967. I have watched many seasons of Saints' football, most of them not-so-good for fans. I attended several games in the Superdome. I moved to Michigan five years ago to be near a grandson about to be born. Now we have two grandsons. One of the things I missed most was not being able to watch Saints' games every Sunday, especially the year you went to the NFC Conference Game. The next year I obtained NFL Sunday Ticket with the sole purpose of watching Saints' games each Sunday. That was last year. Also, last December my son and I attended the Saints-Lions game here in Michigan.

I enclose two pictures as fan support from Michigan. One picture is of my son, my grandsons, and me just after a Saints' victory two Sundays ago. We are all Saints' fans, even though the two-year-old just knows that the Saints are on our TV each week and what they do is football. The other picture is of a location in Michigan called Hell. Yes, there is a Hell, Michigan. As the picture shows, Hell does freeze over! I grew up with the saying that "when the Saints win the Super Bowl, Hell will freeze over." Well, you can win any time now! I hope that these two pictures show fan support and will help inspire the team and coaches to do their best and make it all the way to the Super Bowl.

Please extend the appreciation of an "old" Saints' fan, his wife, our son, and our grandsons to the entire staff and all of the players for all they have done to have a winning season and for all the good they do for New Orleans. Keep up the excellent work! Keep the faith! All of you make the Saints' fans proud! Continue your good work off the field as well. Thank you, Coach Payton.

Sincerely, as in "Who Dat!"

P. S. I have a sister who is a Saints' fan and lives in Kalamazoo, MI. It's on the other side of Hell.

Teachers Are Human, Too!

A teacher friend of mine and I sat in a Louisiana Special Education Super Conference session one year listening to a presentation that both of us thought would really be interesting and helpful to the work we were doing with students at an elementary school in central Louisiana. Jeff, an African-American special education teacher, and I, the school assistant principal, had worked together for several years. I leaned over as we sat and whispered to Jeff that I thought we could do just as well or better as presenters as the person was doing up front. Jeff looked back at me and whispered, "Sure, Mr. Tom." He gave me a placating glance of disbelief and skepticism. We did not discuss the idea on the long drive back to school or for several months thereafter. The idea was dead, and apparently Jeff was happy with the fact.

What resurrected the discussion was a formal request for presenters for the next Super Conference that came across my desk several months later. Oddly, that was the only time a request got down the chain of command to me in a school. The prior school year I had written a grant proposal for Jeff's special education students. The nearby Tunica-Biloxi casino granted the $500 funding for the proposed project for the special education students. Jeff and his students used the money to learn about African-American achievers in American history. The students showcased their learning in presentations after school to parents, teachers, and other students. I go to Jeff's building with the idea of facilitating a Super Conference presentation about the student projects. I attempt to convince him that it is worth the time to complete a submission for conducting a session. I say I will do most of the submission work. I tell him that we can bring in Cajun-French Carla, the physical education teacher who gives up her daily planning period almost every day to go to his classroom to assist with tutoring students, to be a third presenter for the presentation. I tell him that he will be the main presenter because he, the special education teacher, knows the most about his kids and their work.

When I pause for a breath after excitedly telling him all about what we can do, he looks at me and quietly but firmly says, "I can't do it."

I ask why, and Jeff tells me that he is fine with teaching his special education children and Sunday School kids in his church. But he adds that in front of other teachers and in any other situation with adults, he feels not up to the task—that he would not be good as a presenter at the Super Conference. He says he would run out of things to say to an audience of teachers. I counter with the idea that once he starts talking about his kids and what they did in the project, I would bet that I would have to stop him because of lack of time. I knew that he loved his kids and could talk about their accomplishments endlessly. I knew, too, that Carla would buy into the idea of the submission of a proposal. I tell Jeff that if we were selected as presenters, I would map out everything we would do and help guide him with planning his main talk. I finally sell the idea to him, getting his weak verbal OK to submit a proposal. I think what sold him on the idea of the proposal was that we might not be picked to present at the conference. He did not think that many people would be interested in hearing about his kids and their projects. In a few days, we mailed the session proposal.

In a couple of months, I go over to Jeff's classroom with a letter informing us that we were selected as presenters at the Super Conference that year! Jeff could not believe it. He told me that he did not think there was any way we could be chosen. Immediately he appears to be nervous and doubtful about what he could do. I, and later Carla, reassured him that each of us would do fine and that he, in particular, once started talking about his students could fill several sessions of time. Reluctantly, he agreed to go through with the presentation. We prepared ourselves.

When the morning of the presentation date came around, we drove to Baton Rouge in Carla's vehicle. Jeff drove, hoping to calm his nerves and not think about the audience he would soon face. We arrived in plenty of time and scouted the conference session rooms for our location. We knew that we would have about ten minutes to set up. As we waited, both Carla and Jeff went outside multiple times to smoke to calm nerves. Once when Carla came back in, I teased her that I was going to hide in the men's room and not be involved. She answered that she would go in there and drag me out if I did. Jeff was extremely nervous! He paced back and forth until we were able to go into the room to set up. Once there he went outside to smoke and came back in and started to pace again.

The room began to fill. More and more teachers came in. There were at least fifty persons in the audience for the session. The more teachers that came in, the more nervous Jeff became. But I had a plan. The session was on diversity and teaching of diverse special education students. Carla and I would speak first—before Jeff would. Jeff seemed about to burst with nervousness. I was to do one of my parts before Jeff would take over to talk about the project, its procedures, and its outcomes. Jeff was so tense! I talked about diversity a bit and how diverse the three of us presenters were. I told the session participants that Carla was Cajun-French, that I was a mix of English, Irish, and other ethnicities, and that Jeff (African-American) was Chinese!!! No one—not even Carla or Jeff—expected me to say Jeff was Chinese. Everyone laughed out loud, including Jeff. That broke the tension, and the nervousness Jeff had harbored. He talked about his kids and their project. It was just as I had predicted. I had to go over to Jeff at the end of the hour session to tell him to wrap it up because the next session was about to begin. Jeff's talk was a huge success and was awarded warm, vigorous applause from the audience. Teachers asked him questions and complimented him on his presentation and the student project. Carla, Jeff, and I were tremendously satisfied with the session.

When we went out to the car, it would not crank. Jeff, in his nervous state when we got out of the car, had left the lights on; and the battery was dead. Teachers are only human, too.

Born on the Moon

The presidential campaign song, "Dancing in the Moonlight," blared from the speakers in the grand ballroom of the Universal Hilton in Houston, Texas, as the giant television screens on each of the opposite walls showed the red states and the blue states as the electoral vote count was being recorded during the wee hours of this November night of 2108.

"It looks as if you are going to win the election!" Dr. Tobias Farr exclaimed to Tycho Rebant, the candidate. "If so, you will be the first President born on the moon! That is out of this world!" Farr grinned broadly at Rebant.

They both looked at the big screen on the east wall as a newscaster stated, "Our network now projects Tycho Rebant as the next President of the United States." All around them sounded applause and cheering from those at the headquarters of the campaign.

Rebant and Farr worked their way through the throng of well-wishers to the private suite set aside for the candidate, his family, and his close advisors. The two men went into Rebant's inner sanctum for a brief time of privacy before the President-elect would go out to greet officially all those in attendance and face the national and international news media.

"All that you went through to reach this point in your political life—especially the strange criticisms and questions about the Constitutional issue of your being 'a natural-born citizen' or not," said Farr. "Any idiot knows that your parents were American citizens serving on the moon base. That makes you an American citizen. But that issue dogged you throughout the campaign even up to the last week with the universal social media comments."

"Just forget about all of that. The courts ruled for me in each and every suit and case trumped up and brought before them. That just stuck in your craw for some crazy reason. Where I was born doesn't matter at all."

"Yeah. But you know, since you used the word *crazy*, all it takes is one crazy person with that idea stuck in his craw—to use your words—to try to assassinate you! You know that I have always been concerned about such a thing—even though you have the absolute best security all around you," continued Farr.

"You are just a worrier, Tobias," replied Rebant. "Relax. We have gone through the difficult part now. We made it. I am the President-elect. I have plans for the next four years. In just a few minutes, I need to be out front and give my victory declaration. Pardon me for a bit, Tobias."

Farr uttered, "Of course, my friend."

As he was leaving the room, Rebant turned and teasingly said, as he and Farr had done for thirty years or so, "I'll see you on the dark side of the moon!" He beamed a boyish grin at his friend of many years.

Farr sat on the big sofa against the wall that was covered by campaign posters. He smiled as he heard the campaign song music wafting in from the grand ballroom where Rebant and others soon would be standing in front of a crowd of Rebant supporters. Farr was feeling "warm and right" just as the campaign song said. He basked in the warmth of being the President-elect's best friend from childhood to now. He did not regret his decision to take leave from his university biometric research and teaching position to become an advisor to Tycho Rebant. While waiting for the President-elect, Tobias reflected on their friendship which had begun more than thirty-five years ago. Tobias and Tycho had attended the same public schools and graduated at the same time. Both had gone to the same undergraduate school but had parted ways for graduate school. They had remained close throughout graduate school, visiting each other as often as possible. Tobias had married and divorced during this time. Tycho was still unmarried. They had re-stoked their friendship in Texas where Tycho entered politics with Tobias volunteering as a political advisor. Tycho had that charisma, that something about him that everyone liked. Everyone always commented that Tycho was so human, so likable, so lovable, so authentic. That's why he won he thought. Tobias felt so good about the future, and he would be one who would be helping with what the future would be. He chuckled to himself at the thought of their often-repeated phrase about seeing the other person on the dark side of the moon. It had first been said by Tycho the first day they had met each other in elementary school when the bell rang to go home. The two of them made it their catch-phrase for life.

Farr reached into his coat pocket to retrieve his PING communication device, his Personal Interactive Neurological Generator. He said aloud its name "Starla" to activate it. He spoke other commands that PING responded to with various screens. He looked and listened to the latest election news and grinned broadly. He let out a long breath.

Tycho came back into the room after freshening up and said to his friend, "Are you ready? I am. Let's go."

The two men began moving to the grand ballroom for the official speech and celebration. They heard the campaign song again. They saw people dancing and applauding. Now the supporters and reporters focused their attention on Tycho Rebant, the person of the hour.

The person of the hour became the person of the year twice in his first term as President. In the second term he again was person of the year another time. Times were good—better than good. But in the second year of the second administration, things changed. Or, at least, Tycho Rebant changed. Initially only his close associates noticed. The President became obsessed with his own agenda. To most people it seemed that he wanted a certain legacy.

Tobias Farr first began to notice that President Tycho Rebant seemed constantly irritable and disagreeable when anyone attempted to counter him in the pursuit of his agenda. The President seemed driven both professionally and personally and expended all his time and energy to complete his goals. Rebant advocated and promoted twin objectives—expanding and updating the military and expanding and updating the space and undersea programs. He promoted an intertwining of both programs in order to enhance each.

For the military, President Rebant approved new technological satellite weaponry, increased military personnel, increased maintenance funds, re-opened a dozen bases in U. S. states and territories, increased infrastructure funding of major interstate highways and key railroads, and ordered a new emphasis with appropriate funding on research and development. For the space program, he increased monies for the three U. S. moon bases, added two more missions to Mars, initiated a new deep-space probe project, began construction of an additional Earth-orbiting space station and another moon-orbiting space station, and added staffing to the space agency. He advocated additional research into health issues caused by space travel and extra-terrestrial living. He called for additional money for oceanography research and undersea biospheres.

Opposition to the President's programs came in the form of complaints about expanding budgets, increasing national debt, and irresponsible spending. Rebant's opponents pointed out that the world had little strife or discord to warrant his military spending increases and elaborate, expensive projects. The opposition voiced its disapproval of too much spending for space explorations.

Rebant and Farr saw one another at least once weekly and sometimes more often. Mostly, their encounters were at formal meetings or at short conversations in the hall or cloakrooms. Only two or three times a year did the two childhood friends meet socially the way they had done in the past. Rarely did the two men meet privately at all. Farr attributed it to the demands of the Presidency and everything associated with the office. But Farr knew that Tycho Rebant had changed—that he was not his old self, not the childhood friend he knew.

Finally, another private meeting between Rebant and Farr occurred. When Farr walked into the Oval Office, Rebant was ending a conversation on his PING VI. He placed his device on the large desk, saying, "Terminus, sleep mode." Farr reached into his coat pocket, hauled out his PING VI, and said, "Starla, off." He dropped his device back into his coat pocket and sat where Rebant motioned him to sit. Rebant rose, came around his desk, and sat facing his childhood friend.

"My friend," opened Rebant, "it is time we talked."

"Now we have the time to do so," replied Farr.

"Remember the cosmologist and theoretical physicist Stephen W. Hawking from the late 20th and early 21st centuries?"

"Yes. He was confined to a wheelchair most of his life," said Farr.

"I can't remember the exact quotation, but Hawking commented that if aliens ever visited us on Earth, the result would be something like what it was for Columbus' landing in the Americas for the Native Americans." Rebant now went silent.

After a long pause, Farr inquired, "Your point?"

President Rebant did not speak for a time. He struggled for the right words. Eventually, he spoke, "Recall how you always teased me when we were young about what happened about the time I was born on the moon? You always told me that I was the only human being born with celestial fireworks as a celebration and that I was to blame for all the communications blackouts around the world."

Farr nodded and said, "Solar flares and no electronic wireless communications for a couple of days. And some of the electric grids on parts of the world were out of commission for weeks."

Rebant continued, "Solar flares and lack of communications on Earth and between the Earth and the moon for more than two days. Unknown to you until now is the fact that there is a direct connection of the solar flares and my birth."

"I don't understand. What does the Hawking's remark about aliens have to do with all of this? Is your obsession with your Presidential legacy of the military, the undersea biospheres, and the space program connected . . . "

The President interrupted with quick words. "I don't give a tinker's dam about my Presidential legacy. I just want mankind to survive!"

"What? What are you saying?"

"Tobias, my friend," said the President calmly. "I choose now to share a burden that I have carried for many years now. I was not absolutely positive of what I am going to tell you until just recently. You know how we used to say that we would see the other on the dark side of the moon? Well, I got hooked on the dark web, the dark side of the Internet. I didn't know exactly what caused me to first delve into it, but I do now. It was a means of communication, a way of reaching me so that others would not realize it. But what I learned from it, all came together about a month ago."

Tobias Farr just listened to his childhood friend.

President Rebant continued, "Those solar flares near the time of my birth were not random occurrences of our solar system. Those solar flares and the resulting communications blackouts were calculated actions."

"Whose actions?"

"The inhabitants of Terminus."

"You mean the planet located on the outer edge of our solar system? The one our scientists were barely able to see with the new telescope we placed on Mars last year?" asked Farr.

"Yes, Terminus."

"You mean it is inhabited. You mean there are extra-terrestrials, aliens, out there? And they are interested in us?"

"Their interest in us, in Earth, has existed for years, even before you and I were born. They were watching us for hundreds of years. They have sent scores of exploratory space craft. They have technology far advanced of what we have, but they are calculating in their ambition to take us over."

"Take us over? You mean they are going to invade and conquer us?" Farr asked.

"Yes, but they have researched and calculated and orchestrated the avenue to do so with the least resistance to them and the least damage to us and the Earth." Rebant continued, "And I am involved."

"What? What are you telling me?"

"The solar flares and the communications blackout. They were a diversion and a means of accomplishing part of their plan. Terminus inhabitants launched a space probe into our sun to effect the giant solar flares and the resulting electronics blackout. That was used as a cover for them to land a space craft on the dark side of the moon for a team to advance to the moon base for surgery on an infant in order to make him an advanced element of their invading expedition in the future when the time was ripe."

"You are the infant?" responded Farr. "What did they do to you?"

"The alien team did what our civilization outlawed years ago. They altered or edited the human genome. My human genome. They manipulated DNA in order to influence my makeup and my future behavior. They did so in order to control me in order to facilitate their expedition to invade and take over our planet. I am a pawn in their larger game," admitted President Rebant. "My drive to increase spending for space, undersea, and military development is what the aliens planned. They want one superpower on the planet that they can control and use to their advantage once their invasion occurs. I am to yield to them and attempt to convince the other nations to do so as well. That way, with the superpower capitulating and cooperating with them, they will have an easier time and can use more of their expedition resources to harvest whatever it is they want. And if the other nations do not give up, the aliens can use our military in conjunction with theirs to conquer with the least cost, if any, to them."

"You are still in their control? But you can't be. You are admitting it all to me," said Farr. "Or, are you?"

"Let me explain some things to you. It is my understanding that the alien moon base mission when they 'edited' me as a human for their manipulation was wiped from the consciousness of the five other humans who interacted with the aliens. The aliens apparently had DNA-engineered their own species for hundreds of years and had developed their own medical and technical science for it. But what they had learned about humans was from a distance and had some limitations they did not expect or predict. In other words, I—their human guinea pig—am a maverick to their science. We humans are somewhat like them but different enough for their long-distance medical science to be a non-exact medical science for them when it comes to us humans. As human scientists argued for years about the unknown and unpredictable consequences that could occur, I in my lifetime became one of those unpredictable outcomes."

"Is that good or bad for humankind?" asked Farr.

Ignoring the question, Rebant quickly continued with his explanation. "When I first went to the dark web, I realized that somehow the aliens communicated to me through it. The way I understand it is that the alien moon mission 'edited' me and established a communication link to me using a connection with Earth-moon communications that I don't understand how it works, at least not with the information I have. Apparently, the aliens 'edited' into my genomes a loyalty to them and an obedience to them. Their communications always re-enforced these two traits as well as provide orders for me to follow. Remember the communications were invariably of a subtle nature in order not to overload their experiment and sabotage their expedition of conquer and harvest. I have increased undersea, space, and military spending and development. I have made our nation into the unsurpassed superpower they desired it to be. I know the aliens have studied everything we have done as far as space and military technology. Some way they can monitor us—perhaps that is facilitated by their early space probes and our own outreach to the moon and Mars and beyond. They can use all the information about us and our technology to take over and make over whatever bases and stations we have to make them user-friendly to themselves. I don't know if they get information from me in any fashion, but I suppose they collect from me as well. I must think that. I try to suppress my thinking and focus only on what they send via the dark web. But, apparently, we have few secrets that they do not know about. I sincerely hope that there is one secret they do not know."

"What is that?" questioned Farr.

"Because they know that I have expedited achievement of their goals they set for me, I hope they are not aware of the secret that their 'editing' of me was not an absolute success for them because of my human nature and that I will turn against them. I am only telling you this because I know that I can trust you and that I need someone to confide in to help me carry this burden. I tried to hold off telling you as long as I could in order to spare you. I hope that I am not putting too much on you at this time, am I?"

"No, no. It is OK. It's OK. I just wish you had confided in me before it became so heavy on you. Thanks. I will help," replied Farr. "What can I do?"

"I need time to push for greater readiness of our military and some innovations in technology. We are not ready to stand up to aliens yet. Even if we form a coalition with other nations of the world, we are inadequate to the task of repelling their expeditionary force to our planet. We still need a few years to reach the point of possibly being able to defend our planet successfully. Let me bring you up to date on some important issues," added President Rebant.

The two men talked into the night without interruption. When Farr left after midnight, he was bursting with information and speculative questions. They set a time to meet next week. They would meet weekly from this time on. As he left the Oval Office, Farr looked at Rebant and said solemnly, "I said I will help. See you on the dark side of the moon!" Both men smiled.

"Yeah. See you on the dark side of the moon!" replied President Rebant solemnly as well.

The next week the two men met again in the early evening to discuss matters. About an hour into the meeting, there was a loud knock on the door and the Secretary of Defense burst in, excitedly talking. The President sharply scolded him, saying, "I said we were not to be interrupted!"

"But, Mr. President, you need to know this news. We received two communications—one from the Mars base and one from the moon base—that each was under attack from some unknown force. And it appears that unknown spacecraft are now entering the Earth's atmosphere. We have initial reports from Germany, Russia, and Australia. You are needed in the Situation Room immediately!" blurted out the Secretary of Defense.

"Oh, God, it has begun. We are not ready for this. The fate of humankind is in the balance. We are not ready." President Rebant looked at Farr as he spoke. "Mr. Secretary, you go ahead to the Situation Room. I will be there in a few minutes. Is everyone assembled?"

"Yes, Mr. President!" said the Secretary of Defense as he left the Oval Office.

President Rebant again looked at his childhood friend and confidant.

Farr declared, "I said that I will help." With those words, he shook hands with Rebant. Rebant felt only a slight prick from the handshake and immediately became weak and unable to stand. Rebant crumpled to the floor all the while looking questioningly at his childhood friend Tobias Farr. As the life ebbed from his body, President Rebant heard his friend say in a low, assuring voice, "I said that I will help. I will help the aliens. You are experiencing a fatal heart attack. The Vice President will help, too, because he was 'edited' just as you were, and as I am. See you on the dark side of the moon."

The President, expelling his last breath, said in almost inaudible words to Farr, "No, see you in hell."

But an Empty Dream

"He finally did it."

"What? You mean that he said—"

"Yes. Barker finally told me what he thinks of me face-to-face. He backstabbed me before, but not he's got it all out in the open."

"Did you say anything? Why did he tell you now?"

"No. I didn't say anything back to him. I was surprised that he would say anything like that at the company-sponsored picnic for the poor children. We were in the middle of a group. I didn't think it was the time for me to open up against him. Not in the middle of people. I was so shocked. I told him that I had never seen him like that before. I asked him what was wrong with him. But I didn't say anything else. It just wasn't the place. Betty's husband heard what he said. I guess I'll apologize to her the next time I see her. It was embarrassing to say the least."

"What made him say what he did, darling?"

"I don't know. I just don't know. I've made a point of being especially nice to him since what happened last year. I've held back my feelings. I've never said anything out of the way to him or around any of his associates. I don't know why out of the blue he blurts all of this out. My first impression was that he had been drinking. I don't know. Wait a minute! I was going to stop by the boss's office on my way out of the building yesterday, but I saw Barker standing by the door so I just went on to the parking lot to come on home. I wonder if he talked with the boss about his sister's boy in my section."

"Did you say anything to him this afternoon?"

"Yea. I went over to him to ask him to watch a group of boys across the way from where he was sitting. I didn't even ask him to get up or move—just to watch the group while we others supervised another area of the playground. Then he said it. He just blurted out some crude, offensive comments about me in particular and about anyone in general who possesses loyalty to the boss. I'm not going to repeat to you his exact words. They were not something I want you to hear. It gets me! It really gets me! But I didn't respond. I didn't lose my temper. What he said I expect from a kid. Not from an adult. I was wondering when he would bring things out in the open, though."

"Has he, darling? You said you were in a group, but only Betty's husband heard. He'll probably keep it to himself, won't he?"

"You're right. Paul has nothing to do with the company. I guess one other person will have to know. I'll have to tell the boss since he asked me to be there the time he couldn't be there himself. It will be to my advantage to let the boss know the facts in case that certain member of the board of directors gets information from someone else. I wonder when that guy will realize what really is going on around here."

"He knows who really works for the company and who is just putting in time. He just probably made some kind of commitment along the way before he knew what was what about the company, and now is trying to straighten out matters without hurting the feelings of some people he thought had merit."

"I suppose that you are right or pretty close to it. In order to get on the board of directors he had to do some maneuvering. He's beginning to see things as they really are now. We talked informally the other day. He made sense about the subject we were discussing."

"What are you going to do about Barker?"

"Well, I'll just go to work Monday and not say anything to him. I hope he'll realize his wrong actions and rectify the situation. I doubt it though. In the meantime, I'll just do my job as well as I can and not let it bother me.

What did the baby do today? Anything cute?"

. . .

"Hi, doll. How are my babies?

"Fine. Just fine. Anything happen today?"

"Nothing with Barker. But I did talk with the boss. He made me feel better about the whole thing. He said I did the right thing by not losing my temper with Barker and keeping calm. The boss surely is a good man. I can't see how anyone can't be loyal to him. He's always there with good advice and help if needed."

. . .

"Barker told me today why he said what he did. He came into my office area when no one was around and put me down again. He began by saying that I had treated his sister's boy unfairly. I tried to explain that if a person works, he'll do all right under me; but if he doesn't, problems will arise. But he wouldn't listen. I couldn't get a word in edgewise. I finally was able to tell him that it was useless to try to talk with him. He kept on and on. He wouldn't let me say hardly anything. Then he condemned me for my loyalty to the boss again. He said that I had hurt myself in the company and with our customers because I had accepted the temporary position last spring. He implied that he was the man for the permanent position because he had more years in the company. He kept on and on."

"Did you lose your temper?"

"No. Believe it or not, I didn't. I felt sorry for him because of the way he acted and what he said. I couldn't lower myself to that level. I really felt sorry for him. But now my sorrow for him has evolved into anger and disbelief that I didn't tell him what I really think of him."

"I know why you didn't lose your temper and tell him off, darling. You are not that type. You don't like to make scenes. And then you tend to be too nice to people at times and think of them before you think of yourself. It's your upbringing and religious ties to your childhood. But when you get enough and when you get pushed to your limit, you'll voice your opinion."

"And there's another reason. I think that my professionalism enters the picture. That, and my belief that good work will eventually be recognized and rewarded. Also, if I keep my mouth shut, others may eventually realize what the other guy has done or is trying to do."

"I hope so."

. . .

"Guess what? Mr. Wilson of the board of directors talked with me tonight after the meeting I attended. He came up to me and said we needed to talk in private. While my friend Louis talked with someone else, I talked with Mr. Wilson. He asked me what was this longstanding feud between Barker and me and what did I have going on. I told him that I did not have anything going on, but apparently Barker did. Then I told him exactly what happened and what Barker told me to my face. He said that several employees called him about what had happened. I told him that something was funny because only three people knew about the incidents at which Barker had said something to me and that the three people were Barker, the boss, and I. Apparently, Barker had gotten several people to call. Barker had spread things. Mr. Wilson said he was going to talk with the boss soon. Maybe matters will be cleared. It makes me angry to know that Barker is backstabbing me again."

"Don't lose your temper. I know that you're being pushed and treated unfairly. Your boss will give you fair treatment. Don't worry. I know that you have been under stress and have been worrying about all this, even though you haven't let on to me. I can tell. I know you. Don't worry. Everything will be all right. You're going the right way. Be calm. Sooner or later everyone will understand the whole situation."

"You are right. You know, when I was a little boy and in my early teens, I read about the scramble up the so-called ladder, but I didn't really think all that junk was true. I thought that good work would be recognized and that workers with merit would be advanced. I guess I still cling to that old belief. I must. But it is becoming more and more difficult to hold on to and really believe in. I can't afford to become disillusioned, but—I. Well, just look at me. Here I am in my late twenties, and what have I got to show for my college education and seven years of hard work for the company? Very little. My mother did want me to become a doctor or a lawyer, didn't she? Maybe I—no, I got into this business because I wanted to. Oh, I've got to wait to see what is going to happen about all this before I say too much else. I wonder what will happen."

"Don't let it get you down. Mr. Wilson's actions seem to favor Barker, but remember what we have talked about before. People recognize all the things that you have done for the company. They know that you have initiated new programs and have been the workhorse in your section. Don't worry too much. Continue to do your job and don't worry about the future."

"Thanks, Alice. I needed to talk—to release my tensions and emotions. I love you. You're sweet."

. . .

"Hi, Baby. Everything's on an even keel."

. . .

"The boss was out today. His secretary said he was sick. All else is fine. I even told Barker today that I would give his nephew some extra help and advice about his job. You know, I can't hold anything against the young man that his uncle does or says. I'll help for several days. Maybe things will defrost in Barker's mind.

. . .

"Bad news. I heard that the boss is very sick. He'll be out for a time."

. . .

"Mr. Wilson was around today. I suppose he is worried about our department because the boss is still out. We'll manage until he returns.

Mr. Wilson and Barker held some kind of conference in Barker's area. One of my people told me. Oh, well."

. . .

"What's wrong? What happened?"

"The boss. A heart attack. Last night. He did not survive it. Barker's been named the new department head. I've been transferred."

The Real Story of Jack and the Beanstalk

I am the Giant you heard about. My name is Mr. Giant. I'm the assistant principal at Grand Castle Middle School, and I am going to tell you the real story of Jack and the beanstalk. I know that you have heard that story going around about poor Jack, the cow he sold for some magic beans, the beanstalk, the golden goose, and the dumb old giant. Well, here is the real story.

You see, Jack is really a troublemaking, petty drug pusher with his "magic beans." Jack transferred to Grand Castle Middle School as a ninth grader last fall. He had been a freshman at a big out-of-state high school. I good-naturally teased him when I saw him with the words, "Fe fie fo fum. I smell the blood of a new freshman!" That's my way of bonding with a new kid that has attended a high school before coming to us. It was just good fun.

Well, I tried to be his friend; but Jack, honestly, was a troublemaker from the very start who just would not listen to reason. The second day he attended Grand Castle Middle School he appeared in my office, seeking a tardy slip. He gave me some mixed-up story excuse about having to sell his mother's cow and a delay in selling it at the auction barn. Of course, I gave him the benefit of the doubt and admitted him immediately in order to get the boy into class; so he wouldn't get behind in his work.

Grand Castle Middle School had a football game that same night. You know what? Jack got into trouble at the game. There, as I was helping the band booster parents in the concession stand, I spotted Jack with a sixth grader. I saw the sixth grader, a quite innocent child, hand Jack what looked like money, and then Jack gave something to the child. I walked over to the area where the exchange had taken place. The sixth grader hurried toward the restrooms. I followed him into the boys' restroom. But I was too late. When I got inside, the sixth grader had just flushed what he had bought from Jack down the toilet. Crying, he blurted out that he really didn't know what Jack had sold him, that Jack had said they were "magic beans," and that he was scared when he saw me walking toward him and hurried to flush the "magic beans" down the commode. I believed the poor innocent child. I lectured him on the evils of drugs, told him to stay away from Jack, and took him over to my office on the second floor of the main building to telephone his parents and make notes about the entire situation. The poor child! He was so shaken up because of his encounter with that bad Jack and his so-called "magic beans."

My next duty was to set Jack straight. But the boy was clever and cunning. When I caught up with him, he didn't have any more "magic beans." He told me the story that the "magic beans" were only jelly beans that he gave the sixth grader when he repaid Jack the lunch money Jack had lent him during the day. What could I do? I lectured Jack about his suspicious behavior and sent him on his way. I watched the end of the fourth quarter of the game. I was so proud of our team, the Grand Castle Middle School Fighting Golden Geese. They won by five touchdowns!

After the game I was one of the last to leave the field. As I locked the gate near the main building, I noticed I had not turned off the light in my office. I headed to the building to cut off the light to save electricity.

Well, let me tell you what I discovered in my office. It was that boy Jack! Going down the hall, I heard noises of objects hitting the floor and walls and maniacal laughter. I became suspicious. Then I quietly slipped down the hall, peeped through the keyhole, and saw Jack emptying my file cabinets on the floor. He had pulled books from the shelves. I could see that Jack had entered through the window. He had climbed up the ivy-covered drainpipe outside my office and broken in! Some beanstalk, huh? Keep the old beanstalk story in mind now because I'm going to tell you the rest of the real story. While I was watching as well as I could through the keyhole and trying to find my key, I saw Jack go over to my prized possession, my golden goose. No, this golden goose didn't lay golden eggs as Jack's made-up story states. This golden goose was the Fighting Golden Goose statue given to me in gratitude for all I had done helping last year's ninth grade class.

I found my key, unlocked, and flung open the door. Jack had grabbed my Fighting Golden Goose and was out of the window. He slid down the drainpipe in a flash! Was Jack ever so nimble and quick! Well, I had to get my Golden Goose from that thief! I ran to the window and climbed out in pursuit of bad Jack. He was on the ground, looking up at me and laughing. Jack started pulling and shaking the drainpipe, which I was holding tightly. He shook the drainpipe as violently as he could. Because of bad Jack, I lost my grip, slipped, and fell. I hit the ground with a great thud! I blacked out. The next thing I knew I was in the hospital, flat on my back with both legs in traction. Jack got away. I hope the police catch that thief. I want my Golden Goose back and all those false stories and lies cleared up. You will help me, won't you? Watch out for bad boy Jack! He might try to sell you my Golden Goose or some "magic beans."

Now you know the real story of Jack and the beanstalk.

("The Real Story of Jack and the Beanstalk" was first published in *Expressions 2008*, the literary magazine of Baker College of Auburn Hills, MI.)

Pilgrim Rollo Number One
Louisiana Cursillo #59

Madam Rector, a favor I ask. May I speak?

I must point out that many of us pilgrims have been scarred for life by a member of your staff. It's that woman with her bell. Look at what she has done to us. Look at the effect she has had on us. There's a woman over there with two frogs on her shoulders. There's a man over there with a propeller on his head. There's a man she has made into a Mafia Don. And poor pilgrim #19 will never be late for anything in his whole life. There is even a couple over there at one table who have named themselves Bell. What about me? I was once a reserved, shy man who seldom spoke in public.

Once my favorite American author was Edgar Allan Poe. I liked the poems "Annabel Lee" and "The Bells" and ""The Raven" to name a few. But I'm sure all you pilgrims understand my aversion to the word BELL.

I was lying awake in bed last night. I could not sleep, anticipating the bell ringing outside my door. I slumbered uneasily for a short time. I dreamed a dream that would cause any American history teacher to burn his textbooks. I envisioned American history being rewritten by Mona Bell Dullard, uh, that is, Bullard, the che-che-cha-cha.

Some famous quotations were changed.

THOMAS JEFFERSON—When in the course of human events it becomes necessary for one people to dissolve the political bells . . .

NATHAN HALE—I regret that I have but one bell to give for my country.

GEORGE WASHINGTON would have slept here but for that bell!

PATRICK HENRY—Give me the liberty bell or give me death!

OLIVER H. PERRY—We have met the enemy, and they are bells!

ABRAHAM LINCOLN—Fourscore and seven bells ago . . .

FDR—The only thing we have to fear is the bell itself.

HARRY TRUMAN—His supporters would say, "Give 'em bell, Harry!"

JFK—Ask not what your bell can do for you, ask what you can do for your bell . . .

DRAFT RESISTORS DURING THE VIETNAM WAR—Bell, no, we won't go!

RICHARD NIXON—I am not a bell.

BILL CLINTON—Paula Jones? No, that name does not ring a bell.

      Anyway, back to Edgar Allan Poe. Since I was already awake, anticipating the ringing and the dinging of the bell, I was inspired to rewrite Poe's "The Raven." I apologize to him. No, not really. I dedicate this doggerel to Mona or Moona or whatever you call that ding-a-ling.

Once upon early morning dreary, while I tossed weak and weary
Over many a quaint and curious pillow of forgotten dream lore
While I nodded, nearly napping, suddenly there came a ding-a-linging
As of someone gently dinging, dinging at my chamber door
'Tis some ding-a-ling, I muttered, dinging at my chamber door
              Only this and nothing more.

Ah, distinctly I reply, it was in hot July
And each separate dying ding-ding bounced its sound upon the door
Eagerly I wished 3 days morrow, vainly I had sought to borrow
From the cha-cha's surcease of sorrow, sorrow for the lost sleep snore
For the rare and balming sleep laden with more than one sleep snore
              Lost to the bell lady ever more.

And the silken sad for certain ding-a-ling sound
Woke me—choked me with fantastic vengeance never thought before.
So that now, to still the beating of my heart, I lay repeating,
"Tis that ding-a-ling lady calling me to my chamber door
           That is it, and nothing more.

Number 19 at the roll count, it hesitated then so longer.
"Mona," said we, "or Moona, truly your forgiveness we implore
But the fact is, he was napping, and not gently ding-a-linging at the chamber door,
That he scarce was sure he heard you." Here he opened wide the door—
           Darkness there, and nothing more.

Deep into the darkness peering, long we stood there, wondering, fearing
Doubting, dreaming dreams no pilgrim ever dared to dream before,
But the night silence was broken, and the ding-a-ling lady gave no token
And the only words there spoken were "I'll fix that!"
This I repeated, and the undying ding-a-ling echoed
           Merely this in nothing flat.

Out into the hallway turning, all my soul within me burning.
Soon again I heard a dinging, somewhat louder than before,
"Surely," said I, "surely it's not the East Beast Bell Lady summoning.
Let me see, then, what thereat is, and this malady explore.
           "'Tis that bell, and nothing more."
To the rollo room I ran and there I could understand.
In stepped the stately ding-a-ling lady quack
Not the least obeisance made she, not a word or sentence stayed she,
But with mien of ding-a-ling lady, I mean, the Queen of the Outback
I know because Dan or Don had caught some flack
           Stopped, with bell cocked back.

Then this ding-dong dandy beguiling my fear/fancy into smiling
By the crazy face decorum of the countenance she wore,
"Though thy knees be carpet-burned and sore
Ghastly, grim ding-a-ling lady, wandering the East Building floor
Tell me when we may sleep on first and second floor,"
        Quoth that ding-a-ling, "Nevermore."

Much I marveled at the bell lady's untimely words to hear discourse so plainly.
While her answer full of meaning—little sleep for sure.
But I said, "Sleep is good; it's where it's at!"
All the pilgrims agree with me as before.
But the East Beast Bell Ringer glared at me.
        Quoth the ding-a-ling, "Nevermore!"

"You must pronounce Cursillo," she did announce.
One by one some of us did try to articulate some more.
But we said *Caruso, Cabrillo, Cabildo* and even sounds more flat,
The Bell Lady arose and swaggered across the floor.
        Quoth she, "I'll fix that!"

Fear, ever here, fear, ever here at mispronouncing it ever near
Would make our mouths and our tongues go "oh" and "ah"
But some of us pilgrims took this Moona with a grain of salt
Because we thought of all the cha-cha,
        the Bell Lady was the only one "da-da."

The East Beast Bell Ringer excelled at her job
That we were all woke up when to our hall she came
We thought she thought she was Quasimodo playing the bell game at
The Paris Cathedral of Notre Dame
Looking at her you can't believe her pitiful lot:
        Quoth we, "Esmerelda, she's not!"

But yet the ding-a-ling still beguiling our fancy into smiling
When to the Mafia Don she pleaded not to be moved to Spartica
And he only mused silently at the wretched ding-a-ling and
Then smiled as only a Don can smile
                Quoth he, "Not Spartica, but Antarctica!"

Then, methought, on the third night the hours grew shorter
Because when the bell sounded I hit the floor.
"Ding-a-ling lady," I cried, as my eyelids dropped from sleep so short,
"This day is the last," I smugly thought
But I see in continuing dreams the nightmare of the ding-a-ling lady
                Lasting forevermore!

      We pilgrims took up a collection and got the bell lady a bell to match her IQ. This we present with all our love and admiration to the one we call MOONA BELLE.

341 Acres

The sun baked the barren fields. Clouds of dust billowed from the wheels of the car as we drove along the clod-strewn dirt road. We stopped. We left the car and jumped a dry ditch onto the edge of the field. We surveyed the level land with our eyes, noting here and there in the distance were puffs of thick, black diesel smoke belched upward into the cloudless sky from tractors which were only specks against the horizon.

I broke away from the group to go talk with my brother-in-law who was on a tractor nearing the end of the field about a hundred yards down the road. The sun's rays were hot upon the back of my neck. As I ambled along the hard dirt road, my eyes scanned my surroundings once more. No birds, no animals, no insects did I see. The nearest trees were in the distance. The land had been completely cleared; not a single tree or bush was standing in the area. The land was void of vivid color. Brown dust and dirt dominated everything. The only shade was that of a tractor, another vehicle, or a person. Across a couple of sections of the field I watched a truck create clouds of dust as it sped along one of the many roads crisscrossing the dry fields. The trail of dust the truck left behind slowly settled back to earth to await the next onslaught of one of man's vehicles. The ground between the road and the edge of the field being cultivated was like concrete. Only clods grew there. The ground was so dry it seemed folly to believe anything planted there could sprout and grow.

As I waited for the approaching tractor, the rumbling of its powerful engine took dominance of the air. Dust raised by the tractor and the sickening black smoke emitted from the tractor exhaust intermingled in the air surrounding me. I could only wait for the feeble breeze to clear the air.

Unbelievingly, I listened as the tractor driver told me that only a few minutes ago he almost embedded his tractor in mud in a low area in the field he was cultivating and that he bypassed sections of the field because of miring mud. I listened while standing on a clod big enough and hard enough to support my weight without crumbling. Things are not always as they seem I thought.

Soon after this conversation we left, the sun still blazing down upon the barren fields.

Fire Is the Devil's Only Friend

The ceiling fan with its slow rhythmic rotation of the creaking wooden blades stirred the warm, muggy Louisiana air rather lazily. The old blades went in circle after circle after circle.

The college kid stood silently at the doorway, looking upon his father with admiration and a long-held sense of respect. The father, intent on the number-covered papers in front of him on the cluttered old desk, was still unaware of the figure at the door. A scowl formed on his face, and he looked harshly at the pages as he clutched at them.

Jimmy moved his eyes from his father and quickly surveyed the entire office from left to right. Very little had changed since he had been away at college for a few months. The office in the rear of the seed store still had the three old dull black filing cabinets. However, there was a new one, and it was a shiny black. Jimmy noticed it because it was new. But a stack of papers, some binders, and a forgotten coffee cup were resting comfortably on its top. Also, he spotted the old office Bible there. Everything else in the office—the shelves, the old sofa, the small table—was in the same state of clutter as was the father's desk. Jimmy knew that everything was in its own place, the place where his father had put it. Jimmy remembered his father saying many times that everything had its own place and so did everybody. Jimmy's father worked at his best when he knew everything and everybody was in the appropriate place. But clutter was not everything to everybody. Jimmy's mother would ever-so-often come along to rearrange things to a better order according to her and thus start a new order. Jimmy knew that his mother had provided the new filing cabinet. No one had to tell him. He just knew. He rested his eyes back on his father and then smiled the smile of an appreciative son. He now knocked on the door frame. His father looked up and grinned broadly. He rose and stepped forward from behind the old desk to embrace his son.

"You're back! We've missed you. How long is your break, son?"

"Twenty days, Dad."

"Good. Have you seen Mother?"

"Yes, sir. I've been back in town for over an hour now. She's already fed me more than I usually eat in a week and told me everything I wanted to know—and more—about what has been going on around here for the past few months," said Jimmy with a grin on his face as he hugged his father in a manly fashion, which made the older man's eyes sparkle with pride and love.

"Did she tell you about them civil rights people coming in here stirring up our n-----s and messing with what we have—what we've been working years for?" asked Jimmy's father, shaking his head.

The smile on Jimmy's face evaporated and left his lips in a thin line. "Yeah, Dad. But that doesn't affect you and the seed store, does it? Besides, Dad, you didn't say the word *n-----* before. You know how Mother hates that word. And I—I don't like it either."

"A lot of things have changed around here since you last came back from college," uttered his father as he wrote something on a pad on his cluttered desk. Jimmy sat on the old sofa as his father returned to his desk chair.

"Things must have," Jimmy replied. "I noticed KKK spray-painted on the road and on some signs as I was driving in. Has that got here? Some fanatics and fools are around here, too?"

"No fools or fanatics," his father said sternly. He looked his son dead in the eyes; then he looked down at his paperwork, picked up a pencil, and began writing some more numbers.

Jimmy took the unveiled hint that his father was busy with his work and was about to excuse himself when the phone rang.

"Hello. Yeah. Hold on a minute, will you? Yeah. Tonight. Hold on," the father said. There was a pregnant pause as the father held the phone in his hand and stared at his son. He raised the phone again and spoke into it. "Let me call you back, Frank." He put down the telephone and looked intently at his son.

"You're not in college to make judgments about the people here, son. You know why I am sending you to the university?"

"I think that—"

"You aren't being sent there to think, boy. I'm paying for your education; so that you can come back here and take over this business when I'm ready to retire and take it easy. That's why. I don't want nobody or nothing to mess up what I got planned—especially my business. It's been good to us—to you particularly. Nobody's going to mess it up!"

"But Dad! All I—"

His father cut him off again. "You listen to me, boy. The civil rights Yankees have come into our town and stirred up a hornets' nest. Our n-----s—our coloreds—were doing just fine without them. Now look. They organized a boycott of some of the local businesses already. I may be the next businessman on their list. When my business hurts, we all hurt. Do you understand? Do you?" The father was openly agitated and becoming hostile.

"Dad, all this doesn't sound like you. Take it easy. Have you been working too hard lately?"

His father, now silent, began to shuffle papers in his hands.

"Mom told me that you've been putting in extra hours. You're worrying too much. You don't seem to be yourself. I'm back for a time. Let me help you. Everything will work out for the best."

"It will if I can help it," shot back the father in a cross tone. "Do you know that Bob Blake's Cafe burned down just a week ago? The fire destroyed everything he had worked for his whole life. Somebody set his place on fire because he served them Yankees and their Negro friends." He pronounced *Negro* in a condescending manner. "Your grandmother used to say that fire is the devil's only friend. They want to play with fire—so be it!"

Jimmy stood. "Dad, don't get carried away!" His father stopped talking and just sat there.

Jimmy looked at his father, hardly believing the words and their implications that came from this Christian man.

The father was not regaining his composure. "We'll talk later." Standing, he put his hand on Jimmy's shoulder and smiled at the young man, his son. "I apologize for getting so worked up about this. I'm sorry. I regret you saw me in such a bad light. I regret a lot of things I have said and done lately."

Jimmy left the store, walked home, and sat on the porch steps. His mother came out, and they talked about nice and unimportant things.

Later Jimmy called his friend Mary to see if she wanted to take in a movie. She was delighted with the invitation.

That evening after supper, Jimmy went to pick up Mary. His father said some business at the store needed his attention and left, too.

After the movie, Jimmy and Mary went for a drive in the countryside south of town. "The back roads haven't changed much, have they, Mary?"

"No, Jimmy. Lovers' lanes are still where you find them," Mary replied with a silly smile as they drove on.

Jimmy turned down a secluded stretch of country road. It was graveled, but not very well. When he stopped his car, the dust that had been following the car engulfed it momentarily. Jimmy had stopped on a section of road that was enshrouded by cottonwood trees. The car was effectively hidden unless another vehicle came on the road behind or in front of them. Jimmy reached quickly to roll up his window to prevent much more dust from getting inside his car. In a moment he rolled the glass back down and said, "I'll bet the mosquitoes are biting tonight,

Mary." He smiled at her. "They haven't had the chance to feast on this Louisiana boy for several months now. My blood is thick from that Yankee cold winter. The first one to bite me will sure go get all his brothers and sisters and cousins and uncles and aunts."

"Will you just hush your mouth, James Stevens?" said Mary as she moved closer to him on the seat. "I haven't seen you in months, and all you want to do is talk about mosquitoes and their relatives." She kissed him on the side of his face. He turned to look at her, and she kissed him on the lips. "Now that should set you to buzzing, Mr. Mosquito Man." She snuggled even closer.

They gazed up at the new moon, which showed itself through the trees. Neither said anything for a while.

"Mary."

"Yes."

"What's happening here at home? Dad is in a big uproar because of the fire at Bob Blake's Cafe and the Yankee civil rights workers and the Negroes. What's going on with all the people around here?"

Mary didn't answer for a time. Then she said, "You know, Jimmy, I think they don't want to change. They and all of the rest of us are afraid of the changes that are happening. Things are uncertain. People are scared."

"But change is inevitable. They can't stop it. Whether it's good or bad or to their liking or not," said Jimmy.

"The older folks are set in their ways. They have lived with things as they are for years. They see no reason to change. They're comfortable with the old and fearful of the new."

"I suppose you're right, Mary. I was apprehensive about going off to college in the North. It was quite a change for me. And sometimes I'm still uncomfortable with it myself."

"You see, Jimmy, you can understand our parents and the other adults. None of them wants change. They want the coloreds in their place. If not, that's the unknown, a frightening change. It's tradition. It's part of the natural order to them. The coloreds used to be slaves. Generations of white southerners will always remember that. Whites will resist change. I've heard the men talking. Some become so angry with the Yankee outsiders. They call them troublemakers and tell them to go home, to get out of the South where they don't belong. My daddy gets so mad, so red in the face. I dare not even talk about the subject with him. What my daddy needs—and the other older people, too—is time. Change needs to be slower for them. They need more time to accept the change."

"But what about the Klan and its reputation for violent action?"

"Aw, Jimmy, that's history. Now the men in the Klan just use it to vent their anger over the situation. They just go out and burn a cross and shout and spout off and then go home. Their bark is worse than their bite. Most of them show up for church on Sunday morning. Heck, my daddy's probably one of them. And your nice daddy is probably one of them, too."

"You think so? My dad never was a joiner. He stays home except for working and church and fishing." He paused. "You think everything will turn out all right?"

Mary mused, "Tradition is a difficult thing to break. But everything changes. We have different attitudes, maybe just slightly different, but different all the same from our parents. Our generation will be the new South."

"Mary, you sure sound like you have learned a lot since I last talked with you."

"Well, mister, we do have some good colleges here in Louisiana. And I do attend one of them. The North doesn't have a monopoly on knowledge." She paused. "Besides, I have a couple of Yankee professors!" Mary laughed, and so did Jimmy.

They sat in silence again for a time. Jimmy felt a stinging sensation on his arm and slapped at the unseen mosquito, dropping Mary's hand. "Oh," said Mary at his sudden move. Mary heard the familiar buzz of mosquitoes. She flailed her free hand about.

"It's time to move on down the road," declared Jimmy.

"Yes," added Mary. "It's time for a change. But we were so comfortable like we were."

"Point well made, Mary," responded Jimmy, amazed at how mature-minded this young woman had become. "You have impressed me tonight, Mary." He leaned to kiss her gently.

"A lot of people are smarter than you think," she said as she playfully jabbed him in the ribs.

Jimmy cranked his car and moved on up the road to look for a good place to turn around and head back home.

A vehicle with harsh, bright lights approached them. It was traveling too fast. It roared past. Then another and another did the same. The last two were pickup trucks, and both careened wildly down the road.

"The fools!" exclaimed Jimmy angrily as they passed.

"What's that? Up there!" shouted Mary. But Jimmy could only glance at the distance. Other vehicles were rapidly approaching them and whizzing by recklessly, forcing Jimmy to concentrate on his driving.

When six or seven cars and trucks had passed, Jimmy could finally look where Mary was pointing. He saw an eerie glow from a burning cross, rising into the night. The fiery cross, twenty feet high, dwarfed what was near its base. There Jimmy and Mary saw a single truck, a figure clad in white, and what looked like a man in a heap on the ground.

Jimmy turned onto the open field and jumped out of his car, yanking Mary along with him. "My God! That's my father's truck!" Jimmy yelled.

At the sound of his voice, the white-robed figure turned to look at the interlopers. It was Jimmy's father. Jimmy ran to him, leaving Mary standing near the truck.

"Dad! Dad! What are you doing here?" Jimmy saw a great sadness in his father's face. "Who is he?" Jimmy asked, as he turned and bent over the other man. The man had been brutally beaten and was lifeless.

The fire engulfing the cross caused the burning wood to crackle and hiss in a foreboding way.

"Dad! Who is he?"

The father, enshrouded in an unearthly glow from the cross behind him, slowly said, "He was a young man. A young man we felt threatened by. A young man of the next generation—of the future. Of the way things are going to be. We killed him—not that we meant to—but we killed him anyway. He was a young man who thought—who wanted to change things. He was a young man—like you, Jimmy."

The father's voice broke with the last words. Jimmy could see tears running down his father's cheeks. "And I have done the devil's work." The father took a few steps and turned to face the cross.

Mary had moved beside Jimmy and the dead young man. Jimmy felt her hand on his shoulder and looked at her face. He could see her face plainly in the flickering firelight from the burning cross which was about to give up its supremacy over the land. Mary's face distorted itself, and she gasped, "No!"

Jimmy turned with alarm to see the burning cross sway toward his father. His father uplifted his arms, and the cross seemingly heaved itself directly at him with a terrible hissing. Shouting "Fire is the devil's only friend!" Jimmy's father stepped forward to receive the flaming marker.

American Sonnets:
Rapt Withal in the Seeds of Time

Look back upon America just now:
Its seeds were sown by God's great hand.
They grew into American know-how,
But that is just what God, say some, did plan.
What Hammurabi did with his law code—
New-born democracy of ancient Greeks,
And wise Twelve Tables Roman justice showed.
Each seed like these the future grew unique.
A seed at Runnymede was dear for here.
The Mayflower Compact was God's work, too.
Devine intervention with Paul Revere—
The Declaration produced freedom new.
In history America grew strong
The way that God did plan His vision long.

In course of growth, the seeds with weeds did mix;
At times the thorns and thistles did show strength.
The one cast down by God did try his tricks,
But God and country held fast still at length.
Judeo-Christian values still abound;
Universal equality survives;
Equal opportunity is the crown.
Work ethic, firm determination thrives—
America has warts and blights and boils.
Opportunity here for labor sure:
The line to enter, long it curls and coils;
Advancement is the nation's all-time lure.
Its immigrants possess star-spangled eyes—
This nation under God it seems their prize!

Once in a Blue Moon
"In the year 2525, if Man is still alive . . . " (from "In the Year 2525" by Zager and Evans)

"How long has our family lived here, Grandfather?" asked teen middle-schooler Marie. Marie and her grandfather talked as they carried out the three separate recycle containers from their single family dwelling to the curb on their suburban street.

"Oh, as long as I can remember. When I was a little boy, I remember my grandparents living in this house with us. They immigrated here when they were young adults, before they had children," replied the grandfather.

Grandfather pointed up to the night sky. "Look up, Marie. There is what is called a blue moon rising in the sky tonight. I read about it on the world-wide network news. There was a video about how often it occurs and the relative few times when viewed under the right atmospheric conditions the moon truly has a bluish tinge. The report alerted us to the actual sighting tonight of a moon with a blue color in this area because of the atmosphere being conducive to what they called the blue view! Wow! Look at that moon! Isn't it beautiful!" exclaimed Grandfather.

"It's amazing! How many times have you seen a real blue moon like this one?" inquired Marie.

"I'm old, Marie. I have seen this color moon several times in my lifetime. I remember the time I first gazed on a blue moon; it was when I was a little boy; my grandmother told me of her country's ancient folklore about the blue moon that night."

"You have never told me about your grandparents and why they immigrated here. Why did they, Grandfather?"

"I never told you? Well, I suppose it is about time I did," admitted Grandfather as they walked back to the house. "It's related in a way to what we just did."

"We just carried out the trash and the recyclables to the curb for pick up tomorrow. How does that make people move?"

As they opened the door and went inside, the old man explained, "Recycling and disposing of trash did not make them move. It was what happened where they lived because people did not recycle enough and respect the environment enough to save it from being polluted to the degree that living in that area caused persons to become ill and die from the pollutants in the soil, the water, and the air. Climate change was real and had drastic effects on the human population. The average temperature rose. That resulted in many problems including rising of ocean levels and submersion of coastal area and other low-lying lands to be covered with water. Many people had to relocate—some very far away from where they resided. People congregated closer and closer together. Sanitation measures could not keep up with the changes in demographics and living patterns. Diseases spread, even with new advances in medical technologies. In some countries national emergencies were declared. Other aggressive nations coveted the higher, drier land holdings of other countries and went to war over that land. My grandparents were refugees from the war in their region." Grandfather paused, carefully deciding on his next words. "When you get a little older, I will elaborate as to their plight and decision to relocate here. It is an interesting story."

Marie had a perplexed look on her face, but said, "OK. Maybe I can go there one day. Maybe we can all go to see where your grandparents once lived. That would be so much fun. Don't you think?"

"Well, I don't know about that. You know I am getting older and don't travel well, especially since your grandmother passed away last year. She did so much to help me."

"That's an excuse, isn't it, Grandfather?" said Marie in a teasing manner. "All you do is go to work and come home and go to work and come home. That government job of yours is your life. I know it, and Grandmother knew it. We all know it. But you hardly ever talk to us about it. If I didn't know better, I would think that you worked in the United Nations Intelligence Office. You are a spy, aren't you, Grandfather?" Marie continued to tease. "You are like that James Bond fellow on the entertainment network!"

Grandfather laughed and said, "You think so! I don't even drink martinis." He grinned at his only granddaughter. "But I do like my work in the Ecosystem Management Agency. I am very happy that you do all you can do to save our environment by recycling and refurbishing and reusing. You make my job easier."

"It would be nice to travel back to their home land, but we never go anywhere. None of us ever go any place. We have never gone on vacation more than a hundred miles from home. The most fun we have had is when we went to the theme park in the next community," sighed Marie.

"Everything we want and need is right here—all close to us. What's the need to go to any other place? And you have the entertainment network that has all those travel channels and programs to show you all the different worlds and societies that have existed from the beginning of time. What else do we need?" Grandfather posited.

Both mused on what the grandfather just said.

Marie glanced out of the window, saw the bluish-tinged moon up in the sky, and wondered to herself exactly what it would be like to live on the moon, even though she knew it was not really blue. Then Marie said aloud, "I'll ask my science teacher about the blue moon phenomena in class tomorrow, too. Oh, I need to finish my homework assignment now." She wondered exactly what it would be like to be on the moon, even though she knew it was not really blue.

"I think I will finish playing the climate change game on the entertainment network. It is our homework assignment for science tomorrow. We will discuss climate change and its controversies and consequences if ignored. You want to play, too?" asked Marie.

"No. Thanks. I think I will go to my room to read a while before I go to sleep," replied Grandfather. "See you tomorrow. Perhaps we can talk about what you learn in science. Good night. I am going to talk with your mom and dad for a brief time before I head upstairs."

Grandfather went into the family room to bid Marie's parents "good night" and then proceeded upstairs to his bedroom. He clapped his hands to turn on the lights and then gave a voice command for the entertainment news network to activate on the huge screen opposite the head of his bed. The volume was on a low level, the place he always had it, in order not to disturb others in the household. The weather forecast was being announced for the next day and the forthcoming week. But he knew that already, and gave another voice command for the network connection to go to his voice password security for his at-work channel. He mused over his messages and laid out his tomorrow work plans in his mind, while remembering a couple of long-term projects in the works. At midnight he issued a voice command to turn off the entire system.

Marie was at school by nine in the morning. She had to wait until the afternoon for her science class to meet. But she did not wait for class to begin to ask her teacher about blue moons. He explained their rarity and that most blue moons were not actually blue but that certain atmospheric conditions would cause individuals to see the moon with a bluish color.

In class the topic was climate change, and the teacher skillfully used the homework video game assignment to hook the attention of the teens in the classroom. They discussed melting polar ice that reduces sun ray reflection and increases sun ray heat absorption by the larger ocean surface thus heating the water causing thermal expansion and rising seas, smaller glaciers, the melting of permafrost areas that releases methane gas causing a greater greenhouse effect, deforestation that cuts back on absorption of carbon dioxide and its transformation into oxygen, the burning of fossil fuels, the failure to conserve natural resources through refurbishing of manufactured products, and other issues. Most of the students thought that the greatest cause of climate change was anthropogenic—the result of human activity. The teacher even conjectured that climate change and rising seas might lead to great losses like that of cultures and languages. The teacher polled them to see how many would resolve to work to reverse the climate change by changing some of their poor habits and to recycle more. Other students stuck to the idea that climate change was only a natural cycle. Some of them even agreed that human excesses added to the velocity and degree of the natural cycle. All agreed that severe climate change could result in things unimaginable.

Marie anticipated a great discussion with her grandfather during the evening when he came home from work. She could even talk more about the blue moon; she wondered how long blue moons lasted—if they could see a bluish moon again this night.

When Grandfather entered the Ecosystem Management Agency complex, he patiently waited to go through the security corridor, put his briefcase on the inspection beltway for the x-ray device, and stood briefly for the human scan. When given the go-ahead gesture by the security guard he had known for twenty years, he grabbed his case and advanced to the elevators. Unlike most of the employees, he took the elevator to the thirteenth subterranean level. Before the elevator began its descent, he had to swipe his special ID card and stare into the retinal scan just above the floor buttons. He thought that his granddaughter Marie would love to know all about this. The elevator descended, carrying Grandfather downward into the bedrock. He put his right hand in his pocket in which he kept his keys and the blue moonstone that his wife had given him the day of their wedding long years ago. He remembered looking at the pale blue moonstone and seeing the reflection of his wife that day for the first time. It would always remind him of her. He told her on their wedding day that he would always carry it with him. Each time he looked into the polished pale blue moonstone after she had died, he would see her reflection. Each time he put his hand in the pocket that contained it, he would feel the polished surface and think of her. Tonight, if Marie asked about the blue moon again, he would show the moonstone to her and tell her again of how much she looked like his wife, her grandmother. He knew that the blue moonstone would be left to his granddaughter Marie when he died. When the elevator stopped, the doors spread open; and he walked out into the open area leading to his office. He would stop in his office for a few minutes and then go out into the large control room that was filled with electronic devices and screens, computers, and the dome apparatus guidance mechanisms.

His family did not know that he was the highest-level coordinator in the Ecosystem Management hierarchy. He was the sithcundman of the operation. He harbored many of the trade secrets that many of the younger employees in the section did not know existed. He was one of only a few that knew the history of his agency—how and why it was created and what it really did in its operation. But Grandfather was not pretentious nor self-flattering. During the day—and sometimes at night—he just worked here. He did his job. He did his job for his family and for all the people located there. He believed in the value of the groupthink. It made life better for them all.

As his day progressed with all its brief meetings and conversations and dome settings for the upcoming night, Grandfather helped solve problems, dealt with programming issues, and coordinated future events, including weather and atmospheric schemes for the season. Even though he and his fellow workers were deep below the surface, all knew the central mission was the dome and its presentations to those who inhabited the surface. Over lunch he talked with fellow workers in the display department about the night sky presentation. The Pacific Rim volcanic eruptions in the general network news last week would foster another night with a blue moon beginning to wane in the night sky. He mentioned to his colleagues that he and his granddaughter Marie had observed the blue moon in last night's sky and discussed its rare occurrences and causes, especially that of the blue-tinged colored moon. He knew Marie would be delighted again tonight. What they would see in the night sky would be amazing—in more ways than one. He looked forward to going home after work.

That night Grandfather and Marie, after they had discussed climate change issues from her school science class, walked out into the front yard and gazed up into the night sky. The blue-colored orb was there once more. Marie delighted in the sight as she had done the night before. Grandfather, however, was not so delighted at the sight of the disguised planet Earth in the night sky, knowing the dome and its shields allowed them to see the blue water-covered planet, itself a victim of climate change. What he did delight in was the fact that the only climate change on the moon was, indeed, man-made. He put his hand in his pocket and felt the moonstone, a real moonstone. He also recalled the old language name for the blue orb in the sky—*belewe* moon.

Peck-Peck

An old tree with many hollow dead branches stood just across the street from the little red-haired girl's house. The little girl often played outside in her family's yard. Heather liked to watch the squirrels and the birds that came into the yard. Sometimes a brave squirrel played under the carport of the house. Many birds nested in the large trees in the family's yard and flew back and forth from the trees to the ground to catch bugs and worms for their food.

One day the little red-haired girl's daddy called her outside and pointed out a particular bird that had landed in their yard. It was a redheaded woodpecker. "Look, Heather. That bird has a redhead just like you," he said smiling as he picked her up and pointed at the woodpecker in the yard. "It's a redheaded woodpecker."

"Peck, peck," replied little Heather.

"Yes, a peck-peck. A redheaded woodpecker like you," responded her father. "He must live around here somewhere. That's our woodpecker. Yours and mine."

Carrying her in his arms, Heather's daddy walked slowly toward the woodpecker on the ground. The woodpecker was busy trying to catch an insect that was wildly hopping in the grass. He captured the bug in his beak and started to fly back up into the trees, but he caught sight of the man and his daughter edging slowly toward him. The woodpecker jerked his fine-looking red head to look momentarily at the humans nearing him. "He's looking at your red hair and wondering if you are a redheaded woodpecker, Heather," said the daddy. At the sound of the man's voice, the woodpecker flew upward into the closest tree. The bird glanced back down at the humans from the side of the tree trunk. As Heather and her daddy watched him, the woodpecker flew across the street to the old tree with the hollow branches. He disappeared into a hole in one of the trunk branches.

"Heather, it seems to me that we have a redheaded neighbor in that old tree across the street. I suppose that redheaded woodpecker is really yours and mine. We should see him often since he lives just across the street."

"Peck, peck," said Heather again.

"Yes, peck-peck. That's a good name for the redheaded woodpecker," said the daddy. "Let's call him Peck-Peck."

During the spring and summer Heather and her father saw Peck-Peck often. They watched for him in the tree across the street. They saw him there and on nearby street lights. Peck-Peck had three favorite places to perch and survey the neighborhood and, it seems, to watch for the little red-haired girl to play in her yard. One of the places he perched often was at the top of the old tree trunk where his home was. Another was the street light just across the road from his old tree. Heather and her father often heard Peck-Peck pecking on the top of the metal street light casing and drumming out a message for all redheads close by. Another street light at the opposite corner of the family's yard was a good perch for Peck-Peck, too. The woodpecker sat there when he noticed Heather's daddy cutting the grass with his lawnmower. Peck-Peck would be atop the light pole and fly down to catch a tasty insect when the lawnmower and Heather's daddy were on the other side of the yard.

Fall came, and so did some bad weather. One night a storm with heavy winds came. When Heather's daddy went out to pick up his morning newspaper, he noticed that the old tree that was the home of Peck-Peck had been blown down and was across the street. He walked over and moved some branches from the roadway. The section that was the woodpecker's house had fallen and broken into many pieces. He saw no sigh of the redheaded woodpecker. He knew Heather would be unhappy when she found out the news.

Heather was sad when her daddy told her of Peck-Peck's house and the storm. She went outside to see for herself. Her daddy followed her to the edge of the street. "Peck-Peck. Where Peck-Peck?" she said softly.

"Our redheaded woodpecker is out looking for a new home, Heather. It's the same if our house was damaged by the storm. I would be looking for a place for all of us to stay. Peck-Peck is around the neighborhood somewhere. Don't worry. He's all right," replied her daddy. "You know what, Heather? Every time I see a redheaded woodpecker, I'll think of you because you are my very own redheaded woodpecker." He smiled a father's loving smile at his daughter, hugged her, and whispered "Peck-Peck" in her ear. Her little arms pulled tight around her daddy's neck, her red hair brushing against his face. Then he wiped a tear from her cheek. She did not notice the one in his eye.

Within a week Heather and her daddy spotted the redheaded woodpecker flitting about the neighborhood. He sometimes came into the trees in their yard. Often they saw him, and sometimes they heard him pecking on the tree trunks. A smile always came upon Heather's face when she saw the redheaded woodpecker, and a warmth always came into her daddy's heart when he saw the redheaded woodpecker and thought of his redheaded daughter.

Smarter Than Frogs in a Pot

The news blared from the huge entertainment screen on the west wall of the group activities room at the small ski lodge in Colorado. Reporters barked out the news of suicide bombers at home and abroad, aggressor nations in eastern Europe, natural disasters of flooding and droughts, political statements in the 2416 Presidential Election, the cycle of *El Nino* effects, and a new miraculous skin cream to reverse the skin aging process approved by the federal drug agency after only two years of clinical trials. As always, there was more bad news than good news emitting 24/7/365 from the central news channel. The last segment of this broadcast was concerning the alarming rate of climate change. Relevant climate change issues included sea levels and the oceans acting as a carbon sink, glacier size, atmospheric conditions, natural habitats, deforestation, tectonic shifts, and even the fact that China had gone back to limiting families to one child. The segment ended with this haunting quotation from Edward O. Wilson, a naturalist who had lived about 200 years ago: "The race is now on between the techno-scientific and scientific forces that are destroying the living environment and those that can be harnessed to save it . . . . If the race is won, humanity can emerge in far better condition than when it entered, and with most of the diversity of life still intact." Three people were sitting in the large room, being inundated by the broadcast.

"Will that race ever be won?" sighed Elise.

"I would rather win the regional downhill slalom race next month on the other side of Denver!" exclaimed the guy with a broken leg in a cast across the room.

"Yea. I bet you would. So would I," added Colton, who was sitting beside Elise. Colton was nursing a sprained ankle.

"I am so tired of hearing about climate change and its dangers to humanity and the environment and just everything! It pops up on each and every newscast I see and hear. Are people doing anything about it? What is our government doing? What is the United Nations doing? Why, even those big businessmen and international politicians when they go to all those international climate change summits are hypocrites! They all go in their private planes and their limousines and leave great, big fat, heavy carbon footprints all the while telling us to cut back on our individual impacts on the environment! They don't have anything to worry about. They can buy their way out of anything—including guilt!" exploded Elise. "While I have to worry about my little ski lodge I inherited from my poor parents. They struggled with their little business and home all their lives, worrying themselves to death about what effect the climate change was having on the lodge, their livelihood. Now all I can do is worry. I can't even pay the second-mortgage notes every month on time! What am I going to do?" Her eyes welled with tears that soon flowed down her face. "What am I going to do? The good snow is late again this season after last year being a poor year for snow and guests here at the lodge. The bank is pressing me. What am I going to do?"

Colton soothingly said, "It will be OK. I will win that prize money next month. It will go on the mortgage and some repairs and maybe a newer snow machine. You said that booking is up for next month, didn't you? We have set the date for our wedding—next August. It will be a new beginning for us. Things will get better. We will get through this together. Have faith."

As she cried more softly, she said, "I do. I do have faith."

"Let's go out this afternoon on the six-wheel trax to look over the property. The forecast is for some snow tonight. A ride about the property always makes you feel better. We'll go up to the top of the slope where we first met. Remember that time? I almost fell off the cliff point when you startled me. I slipped on the ice and snow, remember? You laughed at me! I had hurt this same ankle that is giving me a problem now."

"You're right. Right about the ride over the property. Not about what happened when we first met. You were showing off on your new skis and not being careful. You were trying to impress me."

"I'll bet he was trying to impress you," injected the man with his leg in a cast. "I've known him since we were in elementary school together. He always shows off for pretty girls! You will have to watch him flirt with the other women after you two are married."

"What a good friend you are, Jim!" exclaimed Colton.

"Oh, I will have him broken of flirting in just a little time after we are married, if not before then," Elise added with a mischievous smile and a little laugh. Colton had lifted her up out of her poor mood. "I'll prepare us some lunch. For you, too, Jim. But, Jim, you are on your own this afternoon."

"Sure. Leave me here in front of this huge screen with all of that bad news. Maybe I will find a hockey game," replied Jim.

Elise quickly added, "Perhaps you can find a special broadcast explaining how we can stop the ever-increasing climate change. You can then solve all the world's pressing environmental problems in a single afternoon." She laughed out loud and projected an extra-toothy, quite silly grin toward Jim and then at Colton along with a sly wink.

Colton and Elise drove several miles in Colton's jeep up the mountainside to an open area and stopped to unload the six-wheel trax from the trailer. They jumped in and headed upward to the first rendezvous location for the couple. Only a light covering of snow had fallen at this elevation. Elise looked around and said, "Usually this altitude has much more snow at this time of year. I am dropping down in that pessimistic mood again."

"Elise, let's stop and assess the situation. You don't owe on any of the equipment. You have cash reserve enough to pay all employees for the season. The bank is your only big worry. We are going to handle the bank mortgage issue and catch up on all payments by the end of the ski season. Your bookings are on the rise. You have lots of repeat customers. The whole place is in pretty good shape with only a few minor maintenance concerns," Colton consoled.

"But what about climate change and all those environmental issues that we hear about all of the time on all those newscasts?"

"The ski lodge is high up in the mountains near Denver, Colorado. What do you really have to worry about? Before you answer, look around you and out at the beautiful scenery," suggested Colton. They looked intently at the natural beauty all around them and breathed the clean fresh air. The sky with only a few white clouds was a brilliant azure blue. A bright sun shining down on the couple belied the fact that within a few hours dark snow clouds would be floating over the area dropping, if the forecast was right, several inches of bright white snow all over the ski lodge property and its surrounding areas.

As Elise opened her mouth to talk, Colton pulled her close and kissed her words and her cares away for a moment. The tender kiss lasted for a few seconds, and the couple held each other for a few minutes longer without uttering another word.

The wind changed from a gentle, cool air current into a brutal, biting banshee in a matter of moments. Colton cranked the four-wheeler and started moving it down the mountain to where they had left the jeep and trailer. By the time they had loaded the six-wheel trax back on the trailer, the wind had taken on the character of the classic Old Man Winter as he stirred up a fresh new snow storm. They reached the equipment barn next to the ski lodge, parked the jeep and trailer, and hurried into the warmth of the main building. The night snow storm covered all with a silent shroud of white tailored to fit by Mother Nature herself. Overnight the world surrounding them had transformed itself.

"Good morning. How beautiful is the freshly-fallen snow! Have you gazed out the big windows to see?" inquired Elise of Colton when he entered the breakfast room. "Is the snow fall diminishing?"

"The weather connection channel says it will stop by noon. Do you want to go out in the snowmobile?" asked Colton.

"Yes. Yes. After lunch let's go out again," answered Elise.

While eating breakfast in the activity room, they watched and listened to the central newscast. One segment highlighted the regional snowfall and the predicted seasonal snow expectations. "You hear? Everything is going to be in our favor. We will get all of the snow needed to fill the ski lodge this season. All you need is faith," retorted Colton.

"The immediate future seems good. But I still worry about the next few years and the climate change predictions . . . "

Elise stopped abruptly to hear the next report centering on climate change and its dire warnings for the future of the Earth and for the future of the ski lodge. "There it is on the government broadcast once again! I do not know what to think," lamented Elise. "Who really knows about climate change and its causes and its effects? What is its history? Probably only environmental historians really know. Why don't they tell us the truth, the whole story? It seems that some people just want to scare others into some kind of action. But what?"

"Why don't we stop being frightened? Why don't we stop being uninformed except for what some people want us to know? Why don't we research climate change for ourselves via the supercomputer information network?" asked Colton. "Let's go out on the snowmobile for a time and then come in to spend the rest of the day researching climate change."

"Good. Let's do just that. Let's make ourselves know history of predictions, causes and effects, controversies, and whatever else is needed to put all of our worries to rest," agreed Elise.

After a couple of hours out in the snow looking over the ski slopes, Colton and Elise came in and parked themselves in front of computers. "I'll do government search engines, and you use non-government search engines," offered Elise.

"That's a plan," replied Colton.

The couple spent hours and hours searching and reading about climate change. Colton, at one point early in the searching, said that he would look at the actual history of climate change, going back to the late Twentieth Century when global warming was the common term used by most people. The young couple read about and were fascinated by pictures and charts and written descriptions of thermal expansion of the seas, storm surges over coastal areas, giant hurricanes, changes in the size of glaciers, greenhouse gases, shrinking of the rain forests, permafrost problems, reduction in the size and capacity of polar ice caps, extinction of certain species of plants and animals, tectonic plate shifts, and scores of other related items. They read, listened, and discussed well into the night. Video and audio replays gave them much information, too. They talked about what they could do at the ski lodge and in their personal lives that could help slow or stop climate change.

Elise finally said, in between yawns, "I really do feel better now that I am informed so much more than before. Nothing will happen overnight, so to speak. But I came across that quotation we heard on the news the other day. Remember the one by the naturalist named Wilson? He talked about a race, a contest, between forces of techno-science and science that destroy the environment and that could be used to save the environment. We must use new technology intelligently when it concerns the planet, our habitant. We will have to pay closer attention to what our government and other nations do concerning climate change and other issues that affect the planet."

"Let's remember what we have learned and what we must do for the future," added Colton. "Now we sally forth to save the Earth!" They both laughed quietly and decided it was time to sleep.

Twenty years of married life later, Elise and Colton still operated the small ski lodge in Colorado. Elise again worried, but this time it was more for their three children's future. The central government news agency now reported on events in a global war over historical territorial claims to lands that had long been covered by water and lost to nations because of climate change, especially global warming, that peaked in the Twenty-first Century. The problem now in the Twenty-fifth Century with climate change was that average global temperatures declined drastically in the last hundred years. Oceans were shrinking as sea levels receded at a fast pace. Men and nations once again marched to war.

Within Me Burning

Her friends had talked her into taking the cemetery tour on this day, March 14, 2008, her birthday, after they had participated in the Natchez Spring Pilgrimage activities. The four young women were all students at the University of New Orleans. Louise wore her favorite bright yellow dress. None of them anticipated what the tour would trigger inside Louise. It rekindled the repressed fire locked up inside her from her past. The graves of William Johnson, who was murdered; the Yellow Duchess, whose favorite color was yellow like hers; and Louise the Unfortunate, who was from New Orleans and had the same name; and the Turning Angel Monument collectively resurrected the demon angst in Louise. After a late dinner, the perturbation inside her spurred her back to the cemetery with the Turning Angel. She had to be there tonight before midnight, before her birthday ended—to see if it held the answer to the secret of her life.

The taxi driver, perplexed by her decision to stop at the closed main gate of the cemetery, had begun pointing out the Turning Angel in the taxi's headlights. Throwing money at the driver, Louise jumped from the stopped cab. She scrambled over the low stone fence and walked briskly in the bright full-moon light straight to face the Turning Angel. The angel coldly stared at her as she knelt directly in front of the middle small grave marker with the angel behind it. Tears streamed down Louise's face. Louise drew some yellowed, creased, folded diary pages from her purse and then half-read and half-recited a confession and regret for causing the explosion resulting in the death of five young persons named Worthy, Booth, White, Murray, and Netterville. She looked through tearful eyes at the five small markers with those names and March 14, 1908, on them. She continued to read and recite the diary's plea for removal of a curse publicly placed on Louise's family the day of the last victim's funeral by an elderly woman related to two of the deceased. Louise wept more intensely and looked up with watery eyes at the angel. Her eyes begged the angel to take the guilt away that she had carried since the day she found the diary pages in the attic. She did not want her future children to have the burden of that family guilt.

Reaching into her purse once again, she pulled out a lighter and then lit the old pages afire and held them up toward the angel's face. The smoke from the burning pages irritated her eyes to tear up even more. The angel head seemed to nod. She dropped the flaming paper pages. She felt a sense of relief. Her body crumpled to the ground.

    The people in the car passing on Cemetery Road saw the angel turn toward them in their car headlight beams.

Mine Eyes Have Seen the Abyss
Revelation 9:11

Down in the mind near the backfill
Where it's barren, there is a binder
Where not even can reach a drill:
For eternal watch no winder.

Man erects and sustains a berm
That for God to achieve breakthrough,
For God to place an idea firm—
Mankind's core sample to renew.

Life down here is heaving, hard, cold!
Quarry we work—quarry are we.
Sixteen tons: Goliath foretold . . .
Extraction from abyss foresee.

There must be a beam through bug-dust,
Through methane and sin actinoid
Where the Four Horsemen seem to just
Make men's minds of reason devoid.

Mine God is there with hoist and cage—
Salvation the gift; but it's spread:
Mankind's sin Satan did assuage.
For Man, "Is the canary dead?"

Wormwood Star

The typed words formed a single line on the page.

WHEN THE UNION RUNS INTO PEMBERTON, WINDSOR RUINS BITS. 1R5O5T6C0—6/18, NOON

The postmark on the envelope was so blurred it couldn't be made out. Duane Cory, throwing the short envelope onto the desk before him, turned the sheet of typing paper over. Nothing there. He turned the sheet once more.

"That's all there is," he said aloud. He recognized his old student number inserted between the letters ROTC—15560. He remembered distinctly that this was the code identification signal that had been agreed upon if he were ever to be called upon by his government.

Twelve years had passed. But Duane Cory vividly recalled the one-hour meeting with the army major and the government agent in the major's office in the stadium office area. At first Duane thought it was a mistake. He didn't plan to work for the government or even continue in the ROTC program. But they explained that many times the government needed the services of individual citizens that had no formal training in intelligence work or no government background. This "non-connection" with government would be an asset for secrecy's sake. Also, the individual's own safety, if there were any danger, would be enhanced because the other side would probably not suspect an unknown agent.

The two men appealed to Duane Cory's patriotism. He remembered it well because when he was at Northeast, patriotism and the military were not popular ideas with many university students there and across the United States. Major Stevenson indicated that he had selected Cory to be approached with the idea of being a "sleeper" in service to the government. Both men said that when Cory would be needed may be years in the future; in fact, it may never even occur. Duane remembered his consent to the idea, his vow to secrecy, his oath to the government, and his code identification signal, which appeared on the note received.

Duane Cory brought himself back to the present by perusing the typed line once more. He realized that he was to meet a contact person on June 18th at noon, but he did not realize where.

He had liked his history courses while at the university and still possessed an avid interest in American history, especially the Civil War era. He recognized that Pemberton was the name of the Confederate general at Vicksburg and that Union troops had captured the city. Vicksburg must be the meeting place. He thought about the military park there. He must seek an answer there as to the specific place for the meeting. June 18 was three days away. He would be in Vicksburg then.

Early on the morning of the eighteenth, Duane Cory drove north out of Marksville on his way to Vicksburg. As he drove, he wondered how he could be of service to the government. The unknown had him worried. Perhaps he would be a courier or something of that nature. No big deal.

He had grown up in the area he was now driving through and was familiar with the area around Jonesville. He decided to travel on the Louisiana side of the Mississippi River until he ran into the interstate highway, and then Vicksburg would be a straight shot across to the east.

On the way he saw several signs indicating an evacuation route. He wondered what they meant and why the signs were along this particular road. The day was bright, and the temperature would be in the nineties by mid-afternoon.

Cory crossed the Mississippi River bridge about nine that morning. He drove slowly to observe as much as possible, hoping to get clues as to his meeting place at noon. He continued on to the national military park. He pulled into the parking area and remembered a class trip here when he was in elementary school. Things had changed somewhat. He sat in his car, surveying his surroundings.

Many tourists were already in the park. Perhaps one of the people he saw would be his contact. Duane Cory decided to go into the tourist information center and seek information just as the other tourists would be doing. He was apprehensive. He tried to act nonchalant, but he was nervous.

He was given a map of the park and a brief discussion of the places to see. Nothing clicked within his brain. Cory went outside and sat on a low bench in a shaded area. He focused his attention on the map of the park. The words from the note went through his mind: WHEN THE <u>UNION</u> RUNS INTO <u>PEMBERTON</u>, <u>WINDSOR</u> RUINS <u>BITS</u>.

Looking intently at the map, he said the names to himself. "U. S. S. *Cairo*. Grant Avenue. U. S. A. Cemetery. Graveyard Road. C. S. A. Cemetery. Pemberton Avenue. Confederate Avenue. Union Avenue." He mused a few moments. "Wait a minute," he said aloud. These words attracted attention of a few people who turned to look at him. He was embarrassed. The on-lookers turned away.

"Here's my answer! It must be!" he thought to himself. Leaving the Visitors Center to tour the park, he would be on Union Avenue, and at one point this road would have Pemberton Avenue run into it. He would meet his contact at the junction. It made sense.

Cory bought himself a snack and a cold drink and then looked around a bit in order to kill time before his meeting. He eventually went to his car and drove out of the parking lot onto Union Avenue. Through the archway to the tourist area he went.

He drove slowly, observing the monuments and markers. Cory wondered what his contact would be like. He probably would be one of those slick-looking secret-service types like those guys that are bodyguards for the President. Maybe he would be an older man who had spent his life in government service. Perhaps the contact would be one of the park rangers.

Cory's palms sweated on the steering wheel. He turned up the air conditioner in his car. He was nervously excited. It was ten to twelve. He approached a junction. This was it. There were a couple of cars on the road. The driver in the one in front of the other seemed not to know which way to go. The car went forward after a momentary stop in the middle of the road.

"That may be my man," said Duane in a low voice.

The car now in front of Cory turned down Pemberton Avenue and sped away. The first car was now out of sight.

Cory drove slowly through the junction. No one was there.

Cory glanced at his rearview mirror. A blue Chevrolet was a short distance behind his car on the road. Steam or white smoke was spewing from beneath the car's hood. The car pulled to the shoulder. An old woman got out and fumbled with the hood but could not open it.

Duane Cory thought that he had nowhere to go and that stopping to help the old lady might be a good excuse to be at the junction when his contact would come along. Cory backed his car along the road and stopped a few yards in front of the old woman's car. Another car passed. It had a family in it.

Cory opened his door and got out. He observed that he could oversee the junction and that everyone who went by could obviously see him. "Can I help you, lady?" he asked.

The old lady had just begun to raise the hood. She turned and responded, "Why, yes, Mr. Cory. I've been expecting to meet you." Duane Cory, astonished at the old woman's reply, took a closer look at her. She turned again to the hood of her car. Cory reached to assist her.

She said in a low voice, "You are Duane Cory, 15560; aren't you?"

Cory looked her directly in the face. She looked old, yet she seemed young. "Yes, I am," he finally replied.

"Well, Mr. Cory, I am Baxter, your contact," the old woman stated. "Help me correct my car's little problem, and then we can meet at the *Cairo* site to talk about our assignment."

Baxter indicated the source of the car's problem to Duane Cory. He quickly saw how the engine had been rigged for steam and removed the water pouch and connecting wires and tubes.

A car passed. Then another.

Baxter said in an old, loud voice, "Thank you, young man. Would you please follow my car to an area where I can get assistance if needed."

"Yes. Yes, I will." He closed the hood.

Duane Cory waited while Baxter got in her car and started the engine. There was a little more steam. He returned to his own car, cranked it, and waited for Baxter to pass by so that he could follow. He glanced at his map of the military park. Several miles of park roadway would be traveled before they reached the site of the *Cairo*, a Civil War ironclad that had been raised from the depths of the Mississippi River.

Baxter drove her car slowly along the park roadway. Duane Cory followed. Baxter was in a blue Chevrolet with a Mississippi license plate, indicating the car was registered in Adams County. Cory was impatient. As he drove slowly behind his contact's car, he observed the signs and markers. Some of the monuments were impressive. The road curved to the left. On Cory's right was a steep bluff. At the base of the bluff was some kind of huge roofed structure. "It must be the *Cairo* site," thought Cory. A prickly feeling went up this spine.

Down the incline he slowly went, following Baxter's car. Both cars pulled into the parking area and into adjacent parking spaces.

Duane Cory opened the car door while looking at the gunboat site. The huge structure was an open-air roof over the ironclad remains that were being reconstructed. There was an inclined red-brick walkway that went to the right and then back to the left and then up on top of a red-brick building of an unusual design and shape. The walkway was bordered by black metal railings on the side next to the *Cairo*.

Baxter had gotten out of her car, walked to its front, and was lifting the hood. Duane went over to her. "We should pretend to check again," she whispered to Duane.

"Oh, yes," he replied in a low tone. "Looks all right to me, lady," Duane added in his normal voice.

"Thank you, young man. I'll be fine now," said Baxter. She placed a piece of paper in Duane's let hand as he completed putting the hood of the car down. "Hand deliver the watch to a man in Marti's Restaurant in New Orleans tomorrow night between nine and ten. He'll be dining alone at a corner table. A small red rose will be in his coat's left lapel. He'll respond to the name Mr. Zimmerman." Cory listened intently. "Good-bye. Good luck. Your country thanks you, Mr. Cory, 15560." With these words she turned, got into her car, backed out, and drove slowly away.

Duane was going to ask about the watch and a couple of other questions but had not been given the opportunity. It all happened so very fast. His mind repeated the key words of Baxter's conversation: "package to Mr. Zimmerman in Marti's in New Orleans—small red rose in left lapel—between nine and ten tomorrow night."

Now Duane looked at the piece of paper in his hand. No one was nearby. He read to himself, "Go into the museum display area to the information counter. Ask if a gold pocket watch has been found. Say that the inscription is 'D. J. C./1981.' Show them your identification to prove you are Duane Joseph Cory." The handwriting looked to be that of a female. Duane looked at the paper again and thought that he must destroy it before he left this place.

He walked from the parking area to the walkway. He looked at the *Cairo* and then up at the museum building. Above it up on the hill where he had driven a few minutes ago he could see an obelisk monument flanked by foreground trees, thrusting itself into the sky. He kept walking, wondering just how important this "mission" was.

The roof over the Cairo seemed ominous. He walked onward to the building entrance. The entrance was recessed in a fashion. Just inside, Cory could see four doorways. There were two doors to restrooms on his left. In front of him and to his right were doors to the display area.

Duane went into the men's room, checked to see if he were alone, re-read the information on the paper, tore it into small bits, and flushed the bits away. He put his wristwatch into his pocket. He then walked briskly out of the room and into the recessed entrance once more.

Thinking that he should act more like a tourist, he paused a moment to look at the large picture of the *Cairo* there on the wall. He read the information displayed: "U. S. S. *Cairo*, Ironclad River Gunboat, City Class, Commissioned: January 16, 1862, Torpedoed and Sunk: December 12, 1862, Raised: December 12, 1964."

"Look at that baby," he said to himself. He hesitated a bit more, looking at the picture of the gunboat.

"Duty calls," he thought. "I should be on my way." Cory opened the door and walked over to the information counter. He looked at one of the park personnel inquisitively.

"Yes, sir. May I be of help?"

"I'm Duane Cory. Has a gold pocket watch been found in here?"

"A gold pocket watch? Uh, not that I know of."

Duane swallowed hard and felt uncertain.

"But I just came on duty. Let me check our lost-and-found box we keep here under the counter," said the young woman.

Cory glanced about while the park employee bent down to check under the counter. He sensed himself becoming nervous again.

"I'm sorry, sir; there is no watch in here," the young woman stated.

Cory didn't know what to do. He mumbled, "Thanks, anyway." He turned away, bewildered at his situation.

"Did you say you had lost a watch?" asked another park employee as he walked toward Duane Cory. "Can you describe it?"

Cory turned to the man. "Gold in color. Pocket watch with my initials and 1981 inscribed."

"This must be yours," replied the man. With these words, he produced a gold pocket watch from his left pants pocket. "It was turned in to me about thirty minutes ago, and I've been too busy to put it in our box there under the counter. Your initials are what, sir?"

"D. J. C.," answered Cory quickly.

The park employee put the pocket watch in Cory's hand.

"Thanks. The watch is very important to me," said Cory.

"I'm glad I overhead you two talking about the watch when I did. You would have gone without it, and we may have had it in the box forever. We must have you sign this form, and then you can be on your way," the man said. The park employee filled out a section and then handed it to Cory for his signature.

"Thanks again," blurted Cory. He signed the paper and turned to walk out of the building. "I was sweating there for a minute," Duane thought to himself. He reviewed his instructions about delivering the watch in New Orleans. As he did, while he walked briskly back to his car, he examined the watch. It was old but fancy. It reflected the bright sun into Cory's eyes. He shifted it slightly in his hand and opened it. There were the initials and the year under them. Even the hands of the watch were fancy to Cory. The numbers were beautifully made on the watch's face. The time was one fifteen.

He pulled his wristwatch out of his pocket and compared the time each watch had. A couple of minutes difference he noted. He was glad that he never wore his watch when he worked or played outside. At least his wrist was tanned, and neither of the park employees had any reason to doubt his ownership of the pocket watch because of a band of white skin around his wrist.

Cory was back at his car now. He got in and looked at the map of the military park once again. He could go back to the park Visitors Center or go into Vicksburg proper. He decided to go on through the park and be a tourist for a time. He loved history, and there was no reason to rush. Perhaps he would encounter something to give meaning to the remainder of his original instructions, the part about the WINDSOR RUINS BITS. He drove on slowly.

Cory reached the road by the Visitors Center and thought about how to get to New Orleans and when he should arrive there. He knew that New Orleans was a three- to four-hour drive from his hometown of Marksville. He had been to New Orleans a few times on business and one Sunday with friends to a Saints' football game. He didn't know his way around well. He needed a map of the city.

There was adequate time for him to go home and then proceed to New Orleans the next day. He could get a map in the meantime. A telephone call or two to friends could produce detailed information as to getting to Marti's there. Duane Cory pulled his car out onto Interstate 20 and looked for the closest gas station most easily accessible; so that he could fill up the gas tank for the return trip home. While putting gas in his car, Cory thought about his route home. He could return the same way he got there—on the Louisiana side of the Mississippi River, or he could drive back on the Mississippi side and go through Natchez. He hadn't been there in a while. Cory decided to go through Natchez to see how it had changed since he had been there last. Cory left the Interstate at the Highway 61 South exit, thinking that the different scenery would make the journey home more interesting than going back the other way.

He drove on, feeling a sense of pride in being a government agent for a short time. He recalled movies he had seen about "sleepers" and "moles." He was just a courier, but it was exciting in a sense. The only hang-up was that he couldn't tell any of his friends. He wondered if he could drive on the Natchez Trace Parkway a while before he would reach Natchez itself. Perhaps he could cut off 61 South and do just that.

Ahead on the highway, Duane Cory noticed that cars were slowing and stopping. He saw police cars. There was one on each side of the road. Cory slowed his car. He stopped. Two cars were ahead of him. Cory noted that the police cars were Mississippi state police cars.

"They must be making routine driver's license checks," thought Cory. He reached for his wallet. While getting his license, he saw that the driver of the car in front of him held out what appeared to be a license. Momentarily the Mississippi State Policeman said something, returned the license, and motioned the car forward. Cory inched his car up to the trooper.

"My I see your license, sir?" the trooper said politely.

"Here, officer," replied Cory, handing his license to the law officer.

"In Mississippi on business, Mr. Cory?" asked the trooper matter-of-factly as he looked at Cory's license.

"Uh, yes, I am. Any problem, officer?" inquired Cory.

"No, sir, just routine checks," explained the trooper.

As these words were spoken, the radios in both police cars blared out some numbers and words. Cory could make out "south of Port Gibson" and "tank truck."

"Excuse me, Mr. Cory," said the officer hurriedly. He quickly handed the license back. "Please remain stopped here until I have turned my vehicle and am away. Thanks." The other officer was already in his car and starting south on the highway. The officer that had spoken to

Cory now turned his vehicle and was speeding after the other car. Both had lights flashing; sirens screamed from each car.

"Must be something bad," surmised Cory. "I'll probably be held up somewhere down the road because of an accident."

Duane Cory drove on toward Port Gibson, the next town. As he drove, he saw signs proclaiming Grand Gulf State Park and Grand Gulf Nuclear Station. Now he realized what the evacuation route signs on the Louisiana highway meant. He had not known that a nuclear power plant was located in this area. He wondered if it were fully operational. He wondered how concerned the area residents were about having a nuclear power plant nearby.

His thought went back to his present job. His instructions flashed through his brain once more. Cory knew he was getting nearer to Port Gibson. Eventually he sighted the outskirts of the town and the corporate limits and reduced speed signs. He slowed his speed. He drove on through part of the town. Soon he noticed that other cars ahead were stopped on the highway and that police cars were partially blocking the southbound lane at the next intersection. It looked as if state troopers and local sheriff department deputies were there.

Three other vehicles—an old truck and two cars—were in front of Cory's car. Cory moved up a little when the old truck turned left and went on. There was another pause in place while the officers spoke to the driver of the first car. This car turned right and moved on. Cory moved up again. Another pause. Longer. It seemed the local law knew the people in this particular car. They talked. Cory heard loud laughter. The car slowly went straight. It was Cory's turn to talk with the lawmen. He eased his car up to them and asked, "What's the problem?"

A state trooper replied, "A tractor-trailer rig jack-knifed a couple of miles south of here and is blocking both lanes of traffic. It was transporting sulfuric acid. There's a little problem with leakage. We're re-routing through-traffic. Where are you heading?"

"Natchez."

"Well, then, mister," piped up the deputy, "you have to take 552 and make a loop."

"How far out of my way is it?"

"You'll drive an extra ten or fifteen miles total," replied the sheriff's deputy. "The loop is twenty or so miles itself."

"How's the road?"

"Fair. It's got some curves and goes through some little hollers and such. After you get a way past the old ruins, some of the new section by Alcorn University has been opened up. It ain't bad on the whole," said the deputy.

The word *ruins* struck Cory. "What ruins?"

"Them old columns of that old mansion that burned down before 1900. Windsor Ruins is the official name, I suppose."

"Windsor Ruins," thought Cory. "Those words were in my original instructions." Cory then said aloud to the officers, "Thanks. Thanks. Anything else I need to know?"

"No. Nothing," replied the trooper. "Is there, Ruben?" The trooper looked at the deputy.

With a chuckle the deputy leaned over to Cory, "Well, maybe you should be careful if you see old Angela walking along that road. She's possessed, you know." He straightened up and guffawed. "That old pretend-witch."

"Be careful, sir," said the state trooper. "Just turn left here and follow the road." He pointed up ahead.

Cory went forward a little distance, turned onto 552, and drove slowly onward, thinking about the Windsor Ruins. He would stop. He had to stop. His original instructions would now have to be analyzed carefully. The second half of them marched back and forth in his mind: <u>WINDSOR RUINS BITS</u>. What did everything mean? Was it a coincidence or an elaborate plan that he had to travel down this road? He could hardly wait to see the ruins.

He saw a sign indicating that the Windsor Ruins were on this road. Cory drove on, a little faster now. This was a secondary road. He would not drive as fast as usual. He would be more careful. He had gotten out of Port Gibson quickly. The road was lined with trees. There was a house here and there. Farther on, the trees were thicker, and he was getting to ridges and hollows and curves the deputy had spoken about. No cars were to be seen by Cory except his own. The road seemed to be deserted except for him.

Now Cory saw someone walking along the side of the road. As he got closer, he saw that it was an old woman, carrying a basket of greenery. She didn't turn to look as Cory approached and passed. "That's probably the old woman that's possessed," said Cory aloud as he went by her. He laughed a little nervous, uneasy laugh.

Several cars going the other way passed him. He drove on. Again, he seemed to be alone on the road. A couple of minutes passed. He pulled the pocket watch from his pocket, held it in his hand, glanced at it, and rubbed his thumb over it. He glanced in his rearview mirror. A red car had come up behind him. "The driver must want to pass," thought Cory. The red car moved out as if to pass.

"He's a fool to try to pass now on this section of this road," Cory said aloud.

Cory slowed his speed to allow the other car to pass. The red car pulled up beside Cory's car. But the driver was not intending to pass Cory. Suddenly the red car swerved and smashed into the side of Cory's car. Cory fought to control his vehicle even at the reduced speed. He pushed down on the accelerator. He dropped the gold watch on the seat beside him. The cars were about to come out of the curve when the passenger in the red car pointed a pistol at Cory. At the same instant the red car swerved again into Cory's car. Cory, in slumping to avoid the possible gun shot, lost control of his car, and realized that he was headed off the road and into the trees and bushes. His car plunged into the trees, hitting several, knocking them down. The car ripped and crunched onward, stopping with a loud thud against a larger tree. Glass shattered, and shards flew everywhere.

Cory's head hurt, and he felt really warm. He loosened his fingers from the steering wheel. There was a hollow ringing in his ears. He reached up to feel his forehead. He pulled his hand down and saw blood on his fingers. He lost consciousness.

"Boy! Boy, are you alive?"

Duane Cory opened his eyes slowly. He could barely make out the face of an old woman with a puzzled, but concerned look on her face. He tried to speak, but only a rattling rasp came from his throat.

"Boy, are you alive?" a loud female voice sounded.

Cory's eyes closed, but he opened them again. His head was pounding.

"Keep still, boy," said the woman loudly. "Take it easy."

Cory groaned. His eyes began to clear. He realized he was still in the driver's seat of his crashed car. The old woman apparently had opened the car door and was checking him when he had regained consciousness. His head was beginning to clear now but still pounded, although somewhat less now. He looked down at his legs. He moved his feet. His feet and legs were not hurt.

The old woman was standing there beside the car, muttering to herself. Cory looked down at his seatbelt. It was unbuckled. His pockets were inside out. "Old woman, did you take my wallet?" shouted Cory as he reached to grasp one of her skinny arms. As he clutched her arm, he saw his wallet lying on the floorboard. "What?"

"No, boy! Turn me loose! Turn me loose!" screeched the old woman. "I jist got here. I don't want or need yore money. I ain't after no money. I was going to hep yew. Turn me loose!"

She pulled her arm just as Cory released his grip on it. She immediately began to pick her way through the smashed tall grass and bushes back to the road.

"Hey! Wait! Wait, old woman," yelled Cory. "Wait a minute. Come back!"

The old woman was almost up on the road. She turned, looked at Cory, mumbled something, and hobbled up the embankment.

"Wait, lady! I need you to help me."

While he yelled for the old woman to stop, Cory reached for his wallet. Some money and credit cards were on the floorboard of the car he noted. There were some coins there, too. He noticed that the other car door was open. He saw another card and a bill out on the ground. The glove compartment was open as well. The papers and other contents were out on the ground, too. "Somebody was searching for something, and it wasn't money," said Cory. "It must be the pocket watch."

The old woman was on the road and walking as briskly as she could with her basket of greenery toward Port Gibson.

"I'll need the old woman's help," thought Cory. "I'll get her and then look for the watch." He remembered that he had dropped it on the seat when the other car had first impacted his car. He got out of the car. He was stiff. His head still hurt a bit, and it bled slightly.

"Old woman," he shouted, "come back." He scurried up to the road as best he could because he did not want to lose sight of her. "Hey, come back. You can help me!"

The old woman continued walking. Cory ran after her, calling out. She turned once to look back at him. But now she walked faster.

He was about to catch her when she turned off the road into the trees. He followed. He put his hand on her shoulder and firmly turned her to face him. "Don't hurt me, boy. I ain't done nuthin' to yew," screeched the old woman. "Don't hurt me, boy!"

Cory looked at her face and directly into her eyes. Her eyes were ablaze with fear. She was obviously quite sure that he was intending to hurt her.

"Don't hurt me, boy. Turn me aloose." Her voice became firm and direct and cold.

Duane Cory moved his hand from the old woman's shoulder. He looked at her closely. She seemed to be in her seventies. Her thin hair was completely gray, and her face very wrinkled. She wore loosely fitting clothes—an old pale blue blouse and a long skirt, faded blue in color, on her skinny body. She clutched a small basket full of plants and a few small flowers.

"I'm not going to hurt you," Cory said gently. "I didn't mean to scare you. I apologize. Please understand I was just in an accident and was confused about everything." With these words, he slouched down against a tree trunk. "Can you help me?"

The old woman looked at Cory a long time before saying anything. She took a step toward him and reached to touch his forehead. "Yew got a purty bad cut there, boy. Let me tend it for yew at my house back up the road. Come on; I show you the way."

Cory stood, and both walked back to the road. A couple of cars passed. "I must go back to my car to get something and see if it'll start. Maybe we can ride," said Cory. "What's your name?"

"They call me Angela," said the old woman quietly.

"Angela?" said Cory with an amazed, disbelieving voice, remembering what the local deputy had said.

"Yew heard 'bout me, boy? Yew ain't from these parts. I ain't seen yew before now."

"Back in Port Gibson at the roadblock, one of the deputies mentioned old Angela lived back in this area," replied Cory.

"What'd he speak 'bout me?"

"He just said that an old woman named Angela might be seen walking along the road," stated Cory, trying to avoid the words *possessed* and *witch*. Another car approached and passed the two people walking.

Angela stopped and turned to Cory. "They said to yew I was a witch, didn't they?" stated Angela plainly and coldly. "What else 'bout me?"

Cory figured that he might as well tell old Angela everything he was told. It wasn't much more anyway. "He said you were possessed and a pretend-witch and implied that you were sort of crazy," responded Cory.

"Do yew believe 'em?"

Cory paused. "I don't care what they said. I need your help. You don't seem crazy to me."

Angela turned and walked toward the car off the road. The two front doors were open as well as the trunk. Cory followed. Even though he felt stiff and weary from the crash, he managed to get ahead of old Angela on the way to his car. "Did you see anyone here at my car as you came up to it?" inquired Cory.

"No, boy, I didn't see nobody here but yew."

"Apparently while I was unconscious, whoever bumped me off the road went through my pockets and car looking for something," explained Cory.

"What's that, boy?"

"They must have been searching for the watch."

"A watch. What's so special 'bout yore watch, boy?"

"It's really special. It was given to me. You don't know how special it is, Angela. I don't really know, either."

"Boy, yew talk in them riddles," said Angela. "What is yore name?"

"Oh, that's right," responded Cory. "I never told you. I'm Duane Cory."

"OK, boy. Yew think they done got yore watch?"

"I don't know. I had taken it out of my pocket and was holding it in my hand when all of this happened. Let me think—I dropped it on the seat. They must not have found it because they searched the glove compartment and my pockets," Cory explained. He began picking up his credit cards, license, and money.

"I wonder if the watch could have been thrown from the car at impact." Cory thought aloud. "It would be unlikely, though." Cory glanced about at the ground around the front end and driver's side of the car. Angela looked, too. They found nothing in the grass and undergrowth but pieces of broken glass.

"Let's look in the car itself," directed Cory. He looked closely at the floor of the car and as far as he could under the seat. No watch. He reached under the seat. No watch. He was discouraged.

"Let me try reaching and looking from the back seat. Maybe it's under here," Cory said. He got into the back of his car and crouched on the floorboard to look under the front seat. He then put his feet and legs outside the car with his torso in the car. He put his hand and arm underneath the front seat and swept beneath the seat as best he could. He jerked his hand back quickly. A sliver of glass was sticking in the fingertip of his index finger. Blood gushed out. He pulled the sliver of glass carefully, and it slipped out.

"What's wrong, boy?"

"Cut my fingertip on a piece of glass," stated Cory.

He reached again. Slowly and carefully, he moved his hand around beneath the seat. He felt some other pieces of glass and the metal where the seat was fastened to the body of the car. He lifted his hand to feel the springs of the seat. Angry at not finding the watch, he yanked the wire and spring network.

As Cory pulled his hand from beneath the seat, he heard a metallic thud like something hitting under the seat. He looked there again. This time he saw the gold watch! It must have been caught on something under there; and when he yanked a spring in despair, it became dislodged and fell.

Cory quickly reached for the watch and secured it in his hand. Raising up in the car, he said aloud for Angela to hear, "This watch must be real important. I wonder why."

"Are we gonna leave here, boy?" asked Angela impatiently.

"Yes," came back Cory. "Let me try to start the car." He put his right hand to the steering column to crank the engine, but there were no keys. "Those creeps!" he exclaimed. "Angela, help me look for my car keys." Both looked about in the car and on the ground nearby.

"Ain't no keys here, boy."

"They must have thrown them away from the car. It'll take forever to find them," said Cory.

"No use lookin' no more," stated Angela. She began walking back to the road. Duane Cory turned to follow. He realized he had a dull headache. He walked briskly to catch her. They walked along the edge of the paved road for a time, and then old Angela said loudly as she left the pavement, "Follow me, boy."

Cory thought they were going generally in a northerly direction. A few minutes of walking through the wooded area brought them to a narrow gravel road. They walked down this lane for several minutes. Angela was silent. Cory didn't talk either. Everything that had happened was swirling through his mind. He, too, was becoming tired. His headache intensified. Angela cut sharply off the road. They were following a well-worn path. Cory hoped that her place wasn't much farther. His feet were getting heavier and heavier. Cory and Angela came around a turn and then a clump of trees.

"There it is, boy," grunted Angela.

Cory looked up at her house. It was an old, dilapidated shack. At one time it had probably been the home of sharecroppers of the area. It looked old just like old Angela. It resembled a cracker box turned on its side. It was a couple of feet off the ground supported by what looked like sections of a large cypress tree trunk. The old house had a rusted tin roof. A small porch was on the front. On the porch was an old rocking chair. There were items hanging from lines strung about on the porch. Here and there were hides drying. On one side of the porch were plants and leaves drying in the sun. Here Angela set the basket that she had been carrying all this time.

"Set here on the porch, boy, and I'll fetch yew some herb tea and then tend to yore cuts," said Angela firmly. She went in.

Cory picked out a spot, sat, and leaned back against the house's front wall. He closed his eyes.

When Angela returned, Cory had already drifted off to sleep. She cleaned and doctored the cuts on his forehead and scalp without awakening him. She put a cup down beside her old rocker and sat herself in the chair. Slowly she rocked, waiting for the stranger to awaken.

Duane Cory opened his eyes slightly. His neck was stiff. His eyes opened all the way now. He saw Angela in her old rocking chair. She was reading something. It was an old book. Cory raised his head from leaning against the wall. He leaned forward. He could see that the old woman was reading an old tattered Bible.

It was twilight. The last rays of the sun were disappearing. Cory rubbed his neck and made a slight sound. Angela glanced up from her Bible.

"How yew feeling, boy?" she asked him.

"All right, I guess," Cory replied. "How long have I been asleep?"

"Quite a spell."

Cory pulled the pocket watch from his pocket. The watch had seven o'clock exactly. "It must be wrong," thought Cory. "It has to be later than seven." He looked more closely at the watch. He held it to his ear.

"Yore fancy watch broke, boy? I'll bring yore tea to boil." She picked up the cup and went into the old house.

The watch had stopped. It wasn't running. Cory pulled the stem to wind it. The stem came loose, and he almost dropped it on the plank floor. That was strange. The watch seemed relatively new, and it had stopped running. The stem came out too easily. Cory sat there thinking, opening and shutting the gold watch. He paused, popping the stem back into place.

He heard Angela making noise from within the house. Now she was in the doorway, holding out a cup of hot herbal tea to him. "Drink this, boy."

Cory could see that she had lit candles inside. He took the old cup handed him and drank. The tea tasted incredibly sweet to his mouth; but after he had drunk all of it, his throat burned for a few seconds.

"What was that?" He pointed to the empty cup.

"Somethin' to make yew feel good," Angela said with a smile. "It was good?"

"Yes. Yes. I do feel better now," replied Cory. "Angela, tell me what you know about the Windsor Ruins. They're close by here, aren't they?"

"Yeah, boy. Why do yew ask 'bout them ruins? They ain't much to see. Jist some ole columns of a big mansion that was built afore the war 'tween the North and the South." Angela sat in her rocker. "I reckon it was 'bout 1861."

"What you know about them may help me," said Cory. "Tell me more, please."

"Folks hereabouts don't pay much mind to them. Must be twenty-something of them columns standing. The mansion was built by a man last name of Daniell. It's said he died rat after the place was finished. It was said to be a grand place. The Yanks used it fer a time during the fightin'. My granny used to talk 'bout it to me when I was a young girl. She said it burned down except for them columns a few years 'fore I was born."

"Is it fenced in? how close can you get to it? Does it have security guards?" asked Cory.

"Hold on, boy. One question at the time."

"Has it a fence around it?"

"There's a single-rail 'round it. But you can git through it easy if yew wanted to git next to them columns."

"How about watchmen? Are there security guards?"

"You mean is there people guarding the place?" Cory nodded. "Nary a one. Hardly no people go there I told yew," said Angela.

"I need to see the place. Can you take me there?" shot back Cory. "Let's go now. Tonight."

"Right now, boy?"

"Yes. Angela. Take me there now. Will you?"

"It's night, boy. Yew can't tell much 'bout it. Them columns is next to fields and some trees."

"Angela, I need to go to those ruins. It's very important. It's really important. You helped me before. Please help me again. I need your help. You are my friend, aren't you?"

Angela looked pleased when Cory spoke those words. A smile broke over her wrinkled face.

"I'll take you in a while. I can gather some roots and such over near them ruins, too." There was a pause. "First I must pray for your healing, boy." She stood. Her Bible was in her hand.

"Come in to the light, boy," she said and motioned him to follow her inside her house. Duane Cory got up and went into the small room. Seven candles illuminated the room. Cory looked around in the flickering light.

Cory was pointed to a wooden table with a straight-back chair. The table held the largest candle in a pewter candle holder. Also, on the table were a tin cup, some tarnished spoons and knives, a bent fork, and what looked like a pouch of tobacco.

Cory sat and surveyed the room.

Two windows, one on each side, were draped with dirty yellow curtains. Two doorways existed—one that they had come in from the porch and one that they could go into the back room. Cory saw an old bed through the doorway to the back. He also saw a wooden cross on the wall over the head of the bed in the other room.

In the room they were in, Angela was at the other side in a corner. On one wall was a metal crucifix. On the other was a faded picture of Jesus Christ. A smaller table in that corner had a single candle burning on it.

Old Angela was kneeling now. Cory could hear her mumbling prayers. She placed her Bible on the table's edge.

Cory looked at the other side of the room. Some kinds of markings and drawings had been placed on the wall between the door and the corner. He recognized a fish, but nothing else. Everything else was meaningless to him. He smelled a sweet odor. He turned to look back at old Angela, who had been praying all the time. He saw a swirl of smoke around her. It had an eerie glow from the flickering candle flames. Angela raised her voice. She said, "Jesus, my Master." She repeated herself.

"Maybe the old woman is possessed," thought Cory. He wasn't afraid, but he wasn't calm now either. Intent on watching her, he saw her stand and say, "Lord God Almighty, help us." She kneeled once more and was quiet. She remained fixed in that position. Cory's eyes wandered back to the watch that was still in his hand. He glanced at Angela. She didn't stir. No words either.

He turned the watch over and over in his hands. "Why had it stopped? And at exactly seven o'clock?" he thought.

Angela was still silent.

The watch was a curiosity now to Cory. The more he looked at it, the more curious he became.

Angela was motionless.

Cory looked hard at the gold watch. He turned it in his hand again. He opened the front and looked at its face. Seven o'clock. He looked at the inscription. Holding the front open, he idly turned the watch face upside down. He stared at the inscription. The 1981 date read 1861 upside down. That was the year Angela said that the Windsor mansion was completed. Coincidence. He looked closer. His eyes focused on his initials and the year. He moved the watch closer to the candle flame. The gold casing shone brightly. There was something different about the engraving. The year seemed to be engraved a little deeper than his initials. Yes, he was sure of it. It looked somewhat darker and more tarnished in the engraved lines and curves than the initials. The initials had apparently been engraved at a different time. The thickness of the lines was different. Cory was sure of it. The engravings had been done at two different times.

Part of the engraved inner cover of the watch was tarnished. The decorativeness was hidden at the extreme bottom arc that was now below 1861. Cory pulled his shirt up. He used the material to rub this area of the inner front cover. He rubbed harder. Some more of the decorative lines gleamed in the light of the candle. But there was something else there! Cory rubbed harder. The inner plate slipped under the facing rim. The inner plate that was engraved had slipped! It was held in the watch's cover by a slight flange on each side that connected to the hinge and clasp sides respectively. Cory turned the inner plate back straight. He rubbed hard again. Something was there. He could see what looked like an *i*, *s*, *o*, and *r*.

At this moment Angela spoke again. He looked over at her. She rose and walked toward him.

Angela, do you have something to help me get this tarnish off?" pleaded Cory. He showed her the inside cover.

"Over here, boy. I'll git it." Angela went over to some low shelves Cory had glanced at earlier. She reached behind some small bottles and came over with a small vial.

Cory tipped the vial on the tail of his shirt. Whatever it was had a strong smell. He rubbed it over the tarnished spot. It got clearer. Cory rubbed more. Holding the watch next to the flame, he made the word out to be *Windsor*! Cory stared in disbelief. Apparently, whoever engraved his initials had rotated the inner plate first. The watch was really old. It probably had been cleaned, refurbished, and shined brightly except for that one area on the inner facing.

"Look, Angela," said Cory, "the word *Windsor* is here on the watch. And so is the date of 1861. What does this mean? Can we go there now?"

"Be patient, boy. We'll go there in a while. There is still things to be done and things to be said here afore we leave," Angela stated firmly.

"What do you mean?"

"Somethin' bad kin happen. We must be ready for it," Angela said coldly. "Evil stalks us."

Duane Cory sat in silence, listening to the old woman. A cold sweat broke out on his forehead. His palms perspired.

"Them law officers yew talked to in town told yew I was possessed and a witch, didn't they?"

"I said what they told me," Cory answered. "But they were exaggerating I'm sure."

"They was right. But they don't know why or how."

"What?"

"Yew see, boy, I am what folks call a white-magic witch. I don't harm no one with my little spells and charms. I try to hep folks that are friendly. I pray to do good. Other folks like me passed down spells and such through generations since afore Jesus lived on this here earth. There's not many of us left. But there's many, many more evil witches and warlocks. They use magic to do bad things and hurt other people."

"I understand," said Cory weakly.

"Yew do not have to be afeered of me, boy. Yew are a friend. I've been restless and uneasy for a time now. I didn't know why. But tonight I know. Somethin' bad can happen. I feel it. A sign was given us. Yore watch. That watch in yore hand is the one that Catherine Daniell give to her husband jist afore he died. My old granny told me of it years ago. Catherine had to git it from the engravers afore her husband's name had been placed on it to give it to him on his deathbed. It was to be buried with the man."

"Was it?"

"No. The watch was taken from the dead man's pocket by the widow just before the coffin was closed for the last time. She was grief-stricken and wanted to keep the watch and have his name engraved as planned. But, it is said that she never let the watch out of her possession the rest of her life."

"How, uh, why did I end up with it?" asked Cory.

"A squabble over things came about on the death of the widow woman. Nobody knows who got what."

"But you really think that this is the actual watch given the dying Daniell?"

"That is the one."

"This is hard to believe!"

"Believe me, boy!" said Angela rather harshly. "Believe me when I say somethin' bad kin happen here now."

"OK, Angela. I believe you. What can we expect?"

At that precise moment, a gust of wind shook the old house. The windows and doors were open, and the wind swirled through. The pages of Angela's Bible fluttered and turned.

Angela went over to the Bible and picked it up carefully, holding it to the pages the wind had picked out. She put the Bible on the table so that the candlelight spread over the pages.

"See, boy, there!" cried Angela. "That is what we can expect!" She pointed her old, skinny forefinger down on the page. It was in Revelations. Angela read, "And the third angel sounded, and there fell upon the third part of the rivers, and upon the fountains of waters; And the name of the star is called Wormwood: and the third part of the waters became wormwood; and many men died of the waters, because they were made bitter."

Old Angela stopped reading. Cory raised his eyes from the page and stared at her. "What does that mean?" he asked.

"Somethin' bad kin happen" was all she said. She left the Bible there on the table, went over and touched the crucifix near it, and walked into the other room and touched the wooden cross over her bed. There she paused momentarily. Then she quickly turned and moved out of Cory's sight to the other side of the back room. In a minute she came back into the room with Cory.

"Here, boy, wear this here 'round yore neck," she commanded. She thrust a small pouch with a thin leather strap connected to it into Cory's hand. Without question, Cory tied it around his neck.

"Follow me, boy," said Angela as she disappeared out of the front doorway into the darkness. Putting the watch into his pocket, Cory followed her into the night. They didn't speak for a long time. The moon was full, and the night sky had only a few scattered clouds. The stars shined brilliantly.

Cory, once when he gazed up at the moon and stars, wondered if one of the shining specks was the Wormwood Star from Revelations. They crossed a paved road once. They followed a lane for a time and then trudged through the dense woods. Cory was amazed at how fast Angela was walking.

They had been walking a long time when Angela turned to Duane Cory and said in a low voice, "We're near them ruins. We're coming up on the back side."

Cory followed. He thought he heard voices. It was probably his imagination after all Angela and he had talked about. His pulse jumped to a rapid rate. Angela turned to him as she walked, "Quiet, boy. Somebody's here. We'll stay in the trees."

They edged forward among the trees. Cory could see the columns now. They were huge. They were like silent giants. Angela moved closer. Cory stuck with her. Inch by inch, they carefully moved toward the columns.

Cory and Angela could hear the voices but not clearly. Cory could discern figures of people in among the columns. There was a large bonfire and a small fire under a cauldron, and more light was emitted by several torches scattered about. The two uninvited observers crept nearer, always glancing at the figures in among the tall columns. Angela moved behind the largest tree nearest the columns. She motioned for Cory. As he crouched beside her, she whispered, "No closer, boy."

Cory silently agreed. This was a good vantage point to watch from. He glanced at Angela, saw that she was kneeling and that her lips were moving emitting inaudible words, and moved around slightly to the other side of the tree trunk. He now directed his eyes to what was happening in the middle of the columns.

The figures were doing some sort of whirling, spinning dance around the fire. The figures were all women, and all of them were naked! They were spinning and turning and whirling. Now they joined hands and moved clockwise around the fire. They went faster and faster and faster.

Cory could see that one of the women broke from the circle, which immediately closed itself, and went over to a low table or something like one. He thought he could see a cross that had been turned upside down. There also was a banner with an inverted five-pointed star. There on the table were a large book, several burning candles, a skull, a chalice, and other items Cory couldn't determine. The cauldron with a low fire under it was over to the side.

Cory attempted to count the women. There were at least ten. He turned to ask Angela a question, and there she was, staring him in the face.

"Witches, boy. Thirteen of 'em. Evil ones," she said coldly. "It's a black mass."

Cory's spine tingled. Angela whispered again. "Them witches ain't from around here. I drove the last evilness of that kind from here forty years ago."

"Where did they come from?"

"I don't rightly know."

"I'm moving in closer."

"No, boy, don't!"

Cory paid no attention to old Angela. He got on his stomach and crawled closer. Slowly he went. He reached the nearest column. It was large enough to hide him well. He glanced back at Angela. He could barely see her. She was kneeling. He saw her raise both hands skyward.

Duane Cory's attention returned to the witches when a hand bell was rung by the one not in the circle. The others ceased their whirling dance and moved in front of the table that served as the altar for the mass. Each of them knelt.

Cory could see that each had a necklace and some kind of cord about the waist. The one at the altar had a garter on her left thigh and a headdress that was a silver crescent moon. The one in front raised a black-handled knife into the air and said something in a loud voice that Cory did not understand. He reached to his neck and grasped the pouch that Angela had him wear. He prayed to God for protection.

In a low, commanding voice, the priestess leader said to the others, "You have been summoned here to aid one of your sisters in your Lord Master's work." There was a silent pause.

One of the other twelve rose and walked forward. At the front she turned to address the group. She said, "Several days ago an advanced computer chip being smuggled by the People's Faction to a foreign government fell into the hands of an imposter in the faction. She was an agent of the C. I. A. She hid the computer chip here among the ruins or nearby before her true identity was discovered. She refused to divulge the hiding place. She paid with her life. I request that your collective power be utilized to find the computer chip and enable the People's Faction to progress toward its goal of liberating the masses from the neo-Nazi government in this country."

She went back to her place in the group. The priestess spoke again in a low voice that Cory did not understand. She clapped her hands. All stood. The woman that had spoken was put in the center of a circle formed by the others. She stood, and the others knelt in place around her. The circle was about nine or ten feet in diameter judged Cory. Long, low moans and harsh cries erupted from those in the circle itself. The one in the middle lay on her back, her limbs spread-eagled on the ground. A high-pitched whine issued from her mouth. She continued it with every breath.

Cory decided he had seen enough. He began to crawl back to where he had left Angela. The wind was picking up. He glanced back at the witches. The flames from the torches were being whipped about by the stronger wind. He looked up at the heavens. Clouds were massing. He heard a distant rumble of thunder. Cory hastily crawled, looking for Angela.

"Angela. Angela!" he whispered urgently.

No answer. Thunder sounded from the massing rain clouds. More thunder, closer this time. Cory could still hear the high-pitched whine of the witch.

"Angela. Angela, where are you?"

He was back at the point that he had left her. No old woman.

"Angela!"

Cory strained his eyes to look farther back into the dark trees. He saw her. He scurried to her. "Angela."

Angela did not respond. She looked as if she was in a trance. She clutched a pouch in one hand and a small cross in the other. Her lips moved, but no sound came out.

Cory called her name again, but she still did not respond. Her arms were crossed against her chest.

"Angela," he said. "Are you OK?"

Nothing.

More thunder. This time it was sharp and distinct and loud. But there was no lightning.

Cory grew worried about the old woman. She remained rigidly fixed in her position. She muttered something Cory could not comprehend. As the last syllable died in her throat, there was a tremendous flash of lightning near them, a tremendous clap of thunder above them, and a downpouring of torrential rain on them.

Cory saw old Angela collapse into a heap among the trees. He turned to look at the witches. They were no longer there! He could not believe his eyes.

He turned his attention back to Angela. A closer look at Angela revealed that she was breathing in a labored manner but was otherwise all right. Cory straightened her so that she could lie comfortably and then hastily made his way through the trees and rain and in among the ruins of the mute columns. The darkness coupled with the rain made the columns awesome and foreboding.

Cory scanned the ground. There was no sign, not one telltale trace, that he could quickly spot to indicate that what he had just observed had happened at all. He wondered if he had imagined all of it.

The rain abruptly stopped. He jogged back to old Angela, splashing as he ran. Angela was sitting upright now. Her breathing was easier.

"What happened to the witches, Angela?" asked Cory.

"God Almighty drove 'em away from here. He scattered them to the winds."

"What about you?"

"I was able to help the Lord. That's all." She paused, took a deep breath, and said, "Let's go home; I'm tired." Angela stood and smiled weakly. "Yew want to come back here tomorrow?"

"Yes. Yes. I must return to try to find the answer to the riddle of the watch and the computer chip I heard about," replied Cory. "It must be well after midnight," he added.

Angela did no reply. Instead, she started walking back to her home. While he walked, Cory thought about everything that had happened to him since he left Marksville. Back at Angela's house, they slept—Cory on the porch and Angela in her room. Cory had sprawled out and fallen asleep easily, listening to Angela recite prayers.

Duane Cory was awakened by the rays of the sun on his face and noise from within the shack. He got up and knocked on the doorway to get Angela's attention. She turned to him and said, "Mornin', boy. Yore a sight. Yew hungry? Come in and git to the table."

Cory smiled. He rubbed his hand over his face. He needed a shave. He attempted to straighten his tangled, disorderly hair. Then they sat and ate in silence.

When finished, Cory asked Angela, "Can we go back to the ruins now?"

"Yes, boy.

They went the same way as they had last night, but it seemed to take longer. Perhaps old Angela was still tired and went slower. Finally, Cory could see the tops of some of the columns through the trees. They broke through the tree line and were there. They walked in among the tall stately columns. Cory was impressed. The base of each column seemed twice as tall as he was. The columns upon the bases were two or three times taller than the bases. They must be close to fifty feet high it seemed to him.

Cory was hard pressed to remember types of architecture from his college days, but he thought the columns were Corinthian. The capitals looked to be fashioned of iron. Some columns had mortar and plaster work missing, and he could see that brickwork formed the inside strength of each column. The columns in their rows and groups were simply awesome. What a grand and majestic mansion Windsor must have been! Cory knew his imagination couldn't do it justice.

"Well, boy?"

Cory was brought back to reality with Angela's words. He pulled the gold watch from his pocket. Opening the front, he looked at the time it had. Seven o'clock exactly. He was positive that there was some meaning to the numbers the hands pointed to—the seven and the twelve. He stared at the watch's face and thought.

He then turned to Angela and said, "Either the seventh column or the twelfth column harbors a secret, Angela. But where do I start counting?

Cory looked at the ground among the ruins for any indications of the witches of last night or any sign or clue to which column he should examine. Nothing at all. Nothing.

"What are yew looking for, boy?"

"Last night when I went closer to the witches, I heard one talk about an advanced computer chip being hidden around here. It could be buried near a column or concealed on one some way. I must find it. Help me look and think," said Cory.

They started out front and walked to the right. They walked around the outside of the columns. Some signs had been placed by the historic society of the state telling of the Windsor Ruins. Cory read them all. The two looked up and down each column, around the side, and at the ground around each base. No luck. Nothing turned up. No clue at all.

Discouraged, they sat in the middle of the open area to talk. They watched a car pass on the road a short distance away. Cory leaned back on his hands and gazed up at the iron capitals, the uppermost parts of the columns. Some plants were growing out from these. He looked around at the columns again. Some were only bases. He looked at one that seemed as though the top half had been broken off. He wondered what had happened.

"I need to be in New Orleans by tonight. Let's look again, Angela. Look more closely," he said.

"Don't know what I'm looking fer if I find it," she complained.

They went back to the front. Eight columns were in line in the front. Cory walked between the two middle columns. Four columns were in line on each side of him.

Angela walked directly in front of the column on his left as he looked out toward the road. She had her back to the road. She was looking up at the uppermost part of the tall column. Cory saw and heard a car out on the road. It was white. He had seen one like it before, but when? His eyes fixed on the car. It came closer. It was going fairly fast. Angela was still looking upward. She had not noticed the car.

Suddenly, there was a squeal of tires on the pavement. The car braked to a sudden stop. While Cory stood there looking, wondering what was going on, a single figure popped out of the car. There was a sharp crack.

Cory regained his senses just before the noise. "That man has a gun! He fired it!" yelled Cory.

"Get down, Angela!" he screamed. He lunged at her to try to knock her down. He felt a hot stinging on his right forearm. Immediately there was another crack from the gun.

His hand had just touched Angela's side when he heard her cry out in pain. She was hit! He felt a warm oozing. They fell. He scurried to pull Angela behind a column's base. He didn't know what to do.

He heard more shots and a police car siren. Then there was a screech of tires on pavement again. Cory peeped from behind the base of the column. The white car was whizzing away. Two other cars suddenly appeared. The first one was a state police car. The second one was unmarked. The unmarked blue car slowed and turned in on the gravel road leading through the field to the ruins. The police car's siren was still blaring as it followed the white car away from the site. The sound died away soon after the car was out of sight. The blue car stopped within a few feet of Angela and Cory.

Cory looked down at Angela. He thought that she must be in shock. He tore part of his shirt and held the cloth against the wound in her back.

Three people—two men and a woman—got out of the blue car. "Duane Cory. Duane Cory," called out a female voice.

"This old woman is hurt. Help her," cried out Cory.

As he spoke, another police car arrived and pulled off the paved road onto the gravel one to the ruins. Two local sheriff's deputies got out.

"Are you Duane Cory?" asked one of the men who was wearing a suit, not a deputy uniform.

"Yes, he is," answered the female before Cory could answer himself.

Cory looked at the woman. He thought he recognized her voice, but he didn't recognize her. He stared. Her eyes were faintly familiar. He spoke, "I am Duane Cory. Who are you people?"

As Angela was being helped and moved into the sheriff's car, Cory got his answer. The woman responded, "We're with the government. These other men are Claiborne County deputies." She pointed to those men moving Angela.

"We're taking her to a doctor," said one of the deputies. Angela had been placed in their car. They drove away hurriedly.

"She will be OK. Don't worry, Mr. Cory," said one of the men in a suit when he noticed the concern on Cory's face. "You'll see her later. It's a promise."

The woman spoke again, "Mr. Cory, you may recognize my voice. I'm Baxter. I met you in Vicksburg."

"But Baxter was old," Cory said hastily.

"It was make-up. I had a reason for it. I'll explain later. Let me introduce my associates. This is Rick Anderson, a C. I. A. operative, and this is Lee Benjamin, F. B. I. I work for the F. B. I. as well. I sent you the original coded message you received in the mail. Let's get in the car, and I'll explain everything as we go back into Port Gibson to check on your friend, OK?"

"Yes. I'm concerned about old Angela, but there's something here I need to find," responded Cory.

"What is it?" asked Lee Benjamin.

"Well, you may not believe what I'm going to tell you, but here goes," stated Cory crisply. He related all that had happened concerning his car, Angela, the watch, the ruins, and the witches. They asked a few questions while helping Cory scour the grounds of the ruins and the columns themselves.

Rick Anderson, looking carefully at the base of a column, the seventh one in line from left to right from the front, pushed down the grass that had grown up there. "Over here! This may be something!" he said loudly.

The others ran hurriedly over to his spot. He pushed back the grass at the bottom inside face of the column for them. Someone had scratched *XII* on the base.

"A Roman numeral twelve," said Cory. He hastily pulled out the gold watch and opened it. The numerals on the watch's face were Roman numerals. "A possible connection," he postulated aloud.

"We must look closely here," put in Benjamin. All of them scrutinized the area. They found nothing.

"I can't figure it out," said Cory exasperated. "Perhaps there is a Roman numeral seven on another column." They counted seven around and looked closely at that column and base. Nothing was there for them to interpret as a clue or a signal. They looked at other columns, but they found nothing.

Cory and the other two men again looked at the column marked as XII and all around it at the ground to check if there were signs of anything buried or hammered into the ground. "Maybe that column is for the big hand, and since the watch has stopped at seven o'clock, we should guess where the small hand would point and look there," Cory suggested.

"It's worth a try," agreed Baxter.

They paced off distances, looked, guessed areas, looked again, and finally gave up on this idea after an hour.

"Let's go check on your friend," said Anderson. "We'll think and talk on our way."

"Sounds good," Baxter added.

"Yeah. We're not doing any good here," said Cory.

The four went to the car, got in, and drove away from the Windsor Ruins. On the way Baxter explained things to Duane Cory. "You were originally intended to be a decoy, Mr. Cory. I sent you the coded instructions that I knew you could figure out. Rick had your file and helped me. I had intended merely to talk with you at the military park and send you to New Orleans with a dummy package. You would have been in no real danger. We just needed a decoy courier to confuse the opposition. But things changed. On the morning I met you, I received the watch in the mail. An identification code name was on the outside wrapping so I knew it came from our undercover operative in this area. I examined the watch carefully but couldn't find anything special about it, except that the stem broke when I had wound it a little to see if it would run."

"Who is this undercover operative who sent this gold watch to you? What was he undercover for in this area? What does all this have to do with the computer chip I told you about involving the witches and the group called the People's Faction?" queried Cory.

"I'll tell you," Baxter continued. "Here is the story. Our undercover operative is, or was, if what you heard is true, code-named Ouachita. She infiltrated the People's Faction organization in California sixteen months ago. Our people tracked the group to this area with her help during the last two months. It's ironic. I met her only once. She showed me the gold pocket watch then. It was a prized possession of hers. You see, Mr. Cory, she is a direct descendant of the man who built the Windsor mansion. She told me her story when I said that I was born in Natchez. She also said that if things ever got serious that she would send me the gold watch as a signal. Her initials, by the way, are the same as yours. That's one reason why I let you carry the watch."

"That woman must be the one I heard about paying the price with her life," Cory said.

"I hope it isn't true, but I'm afraid," related Baxter. "We have been tracing the Faction because of a missing computer chip. This chip prototype is so advanced that it seems impossible. It holds more information than you can imagine and facilitates processing that information fifty times faster than anything we or any foreign government has now."

"And it's hidden somewhere at the Windsor Ruins," injected Cory.

"From what you say, it is," Baxter stated. "If Ouachita is still alive and we can locate her, we'll recover it quickly."

"Or if we can solve the riddle of the gold watch and the columns," added Benjamin.

"Let me see, Mr. Cory; what else must I tell you?" mused Baxter. "Oh, yes. Concerning the original correspondence I sent you. My code name for this operation is BITS. Remember the whole message? WHEN THE UNION RUNS INTO PEMBERTON, WINDSOR RUINS BITS. 1R5O5T6C0—6/18, NOON. The WINDSOR RUINS section meant that I wanted you to take the Mississippi state side of the river to travel on. I had intended to tell you this at Vicksburg, but I failed to do so. We had arranged to have your progress down to New Orleans watched through Mississippi and through Baton Rouge on to your destination. By the way, don't worry about getting to New Orleans by tonight. That's been changed."

"I'm glad of that. We need to find that computer chip today, don't we?" Cory said.

"Yes. Let me tell you more, Mr. Cory, about the People's Faction. We have been fighting a running battle with it since its inception in California. We were fortunate to stop them from exploding a bomb in the Los Angeles airport. One of their number was arrested, revealed information about the organization, and relocated by us," Baxter said. "We were able to drive them out of California because of him, but we failed to destroy the group. Somehow the Faction obtained the computer chip and has been attempting to smuggle it out of the United States to the European black market. They would have received in return a hefty sum of money and training of some Faction members by terrorist groups in Europe and the Middle East. One of their number left the U. S. six months back and has returned through New Orleans only weeks ago. That worries us. We don't really know what they are up to. Receipt of the watch was my last communication with Ouachita. We thought we had them sort of bottled up where we could keep our eye on them so to speak. We would follow wherever they moved on to. We think they may wind up in New Orleans. According to Ouachita there are only eleven of them. But they could attract more members with money and publicity. That's why we are attempting to keep a lid on things."

"Well, I hope you can break up this group before anyone else gets hurt," added Cory.

They were in Port Gibson now. They found out that Angela had been taken to a hospital in Natchez. They drove on so that Cory could learn of Angela's condition.

In Natchez at the hospital they were informed that Angela was in surgery and would be for a while. They decided to go somewhere to eat. Cory was later dropped off at the hospital, and the others went to check at the county sheriff's office.

Duane Cory, when inquiring about Angela, was told that she was out of surgery and in intensive care. He was told that she was asleep and couldn't be seen for a time. He went down to the ground floor, left word at the information counter that he would be out walking for a few minutes, and strode out of the hospital. He was worried about Angela. No one had given a hopeful report.

Cory walked for a time, looking at the cars pass by and thinking about the gold watch and the Windsor Ruins. He ambled along the side of the road. Depressed about Angela, he hung his head as he slowly walked. He kicked a can, and it rattled forward on the rocks. He kicked it again. This time it didn't go far because of a glancing blow. It rolled about a foot beyond the top of his shadow. The can had some gold color on it. This gleamed in the sun and caught his eye. It reminded him a little of the shiny gold watch.

"That mysterious gold watch," he said aloud as he was about to kick the can once more. But this time he hesitated. His shadow covered the can. He took a step back and one to the side. His shadow was off the can. "That's it. That must be it!" he exclaimed. "I'll be guided by the seven o'clock shadow!"

He hurried to the hospital. Baxter and the others were not there yet; so he went up to check on Angela. The nurse told him that Angela was awake and asking for "that boy." He grinned and was escorted to her bedside. "The doctor said not to be long," cautioned the nurse. She stood back. Cory reached for Angela's skinny hand and called her name softly. She opened her eyes.

"Is that you, boy?"

"Yes, Angela. It's me. I haven't been far away."

"Listen, boy. Remember the Wormwood Star verse from my Bible. Something bad can happen. Be careful, boy."

"I will. I will. You rest, Angela."

Angela weakly tried to sit up but failed. The nurse came closer.

"Remember, boy, Wormwood Star. Bitter waters. Bad. Wormwood," Angela said.

The nurse now intervened, "Mr. Cory, you had better let her rest now. You must leave."

Angela kept saying, "Wormwood. Bitter waters."

Releasing her hand reluctantly, Cory turned to leave. He prayed for her. He walked away from the bed and was just going into the hall when he heard the nurse's voice call for assistance. He turned and saw others rushing into the room to Angela's bedside. Another nurse ushered him into the hall against his will. His vision of Angela was cut off by the closing of the room door.

Cory found a chair down the hall and sat to wait. He prayed. Baxter and the other two men came up. Cory explained what had happened. They waited. Then minutes later a doctor walked up to them. "Mr. Cory?"

"Yes."

"I'm sorry. The old woman just passed away. The trauma of the gunshot wound was too much for her at her age. We did all we could."

Cory sank back into his chair. He said nothing for a few minutes. All were silent. The doctor and Rick Anderson walked away down the corridor.

"I'm sorry, Mr. Cory," Baxter said sadly.

Lee Benjamin told Cory, "We'll take care of arrangements for old Angela. Leave it up to us."

"Thanks," Cory said.

They all got up to leave the hospital. In the car Cory related his idea about the shadow and seven o'clock. They decided to return to the ruins to check his theory. They would be back at the Windsor Ruins well before seven o'clock. On the way Baxter told Cory that the driver's license roadblock he had gone through yesterday was their means of seeing which side of the Mississippi River that he had chosen to travel. By chance he had selected the way they had wanted him to go. Baxter told him that they had lost him for a time because of the truck accident below Port Gibson. The state trooper didn't report immediately in his haste to reach the scene of the accident.

"I still have a question about something, though," said Cory. "How did those men who ran me off the road know I had the watch or even could be connected with it?"

"Perhaps they found out Ouachita had mailed it to me and followed me," answered Baxter.

"But you were made-up to look like an old lady," pointed out Cory.

"I don't know. But these people are clever," Baxter responded. "Maybe that question will be answered later."

The conversation turned back to the pocket watch and the column marked with *XII*. As they approached the Windsor Ruins, Cory said, "It was a good thing you three and the officers came by here when you did this morning. Both Angela and I may . . . " Cory couldn't finish his sentence.

"It was lucky," said Baxter. "We had found your car late last evening and had been searching for you since then."

The car turned onto the gravel road and slowly drove up to the columns. All four got out when the car stopped. They went over to the column marked with the Roman numeral. Anderson looked at his watch. "We'll have to wait for about 25 minutes." They stood and speculated. Cory paced. Baxter paced with him. Anderson and Benjamin leaned against columns.

"Just a couple of minutes left," announced Anderson.

"Let's get something to help mark where the shadow falls," suggested Benjamin. He went to look for sticks and twigs. He quickly returned with several dry sticks and branches.

"It's seven," stated Anderson.

They outlined the column's shadow as fast and as accurately as possible. The shadow fell in the open area among the columns. Cory and Anderson got on their hands and knees at the top of the shadow and began examining the ground. Benjamin started at the shadow's bottom. Baxter stood near him to look.

"Look, here!" exclaimed Cory as he pointed to a patch of grass.

"What is it?" asked Baxter excitedly as she ran over to Cory and Anderson. Cory parted the grass carefully. Everyone strained to see what Cory had seen. They leaned forward anticipating success in their search. Something had punched a hole the diameter of a fifty-cent piece about four inches deep into the soil. Cradled in the small hole was a clear plastic sheet wrapped around what looked like a large computer chip partially encased in hard plastic.

"The missing computer chip!" shouted Baxter with glee.

"Yes. It is!" added Cory in a loud, excited voice. He scooped it out carefully. He unwrapped the plastic sheet from around it. There was a slip of paper under it. It fluttered to the ground. Anderson almost caught it before it hit. He picked it up.

"There's something written on this," he said. "Grand Gulf Plant."

"Grand Gulf Plant? What's that mean?" Cory asked.

"Grand Gulf was once a town near here," Baxter answered. "Now it's non-existent except for a few houses here and there in the general area. There's a state military park over there—north of here several miles.

"I recognize the name Grand Gulf from my drive from Vicksburg yesterday. I remember seeing Grand Gulf on a sign, but something else was there with it," said Cory.

"You're right, Mr. Cory," added Anderson. "I remember. The sign you saw was for the Grand Gulf Nuclear Power Station. I saw it, too."

"Nuclear Power Station!" exclaimed Cory.

Benjamin said, "With the radical fringe group the People's Faction in the area, we could have bad news." He paused. No one else spoke. "But," continued Benjamin, "it may not be operational yet."

"We must follow up on this. This message must be a warning for us," put in Anderson.

Cory handed the computer chip to Baxter as they all walked to the car. "How close is the nuclear plant to the Mississippi River?" asked Cory.

"Not quite directly on it," said Baxter.

"I'm thinking about what old Angela warned us of. Remember the Wormwood Star? The Bible verse mentioned bitter waters. Wouldn't a radioactive leak or spill or explosion result in contaminated, bitter water?" Cory said.

"You bet it would, Mr. Cory," replied Anderson. "From here to the mouth of the river and into the Gulf of Mexico. It would be a major disaster for the population along the river from here south. Think of the consequences."

"We should call this in to get some deputies and state police officers over there. I'll do it," Benjamin said. He took a quick step to the car.

As he opened the car door, a loud voice sounded from their right, "Hold it right there, mister. Don't move."

All heads turned to see a man coming toward them. He held a foreign-made automatic rifle on them. "You people carefully take your guns and throw them out in the field," he growled.

Anderson and Benjamin slowly took their guns and flipped them into the field.

"You, too, lady!" he said gruffly.

Baxter opened her shoulder-strap purse and daintily tossed her gun toward the field. It landed with a thud—much closer than the guns of the two men. The man, dressed in jeans and a sweatshirt, raised his rifle into the air and fired a short burst. Then he leveled the gun back at the others.

Momentarily, a late-model pickup truck came down the highway, turned on the gravel road, and pulled up by the car. Another man got out. He was wearing old corduroy pants and a T-shirt. He had a rifle like the other man's.

"You pigs found our missing merchandise for us," said the first man.

"Members of the People's Faction," said Anderson aloud.

"Yes," responded the man who had driven up in the pickup.

"Hand it over, lady," the first man said coldly to Baxter. He held out his hand.

Baxter hesitated.

The man aimed the gun at her. "Now!" he shouted angrily.

"Do it," said Benjamin. "He knows you have it, and he'll kill you if you don't give it to them."

Baxter held out the computer chip. The first man got closer to grab it out of her hand. He smiled as he clasped it.

"All of you get over there," the man said as he waved the gun and pointed toward the row of columns. The other man covered them with his gun, too. They moved closer.

The agents and Cory moved over in a line. Baxter was a couple of feet away from Cory, Anderson, and Benjamin, who were grouping together.

Benjamin dragged his feet and was slow in moving. Cory heard him say to Anderson in a whisper, "They're going to kill us."

The first man, impatient, poked his gun barrel in Benjamin's back to hurry him along. Before Cory knew what was happening, Benjamin had quickly and expertly whirled about and was struggling with the man and his gun. The second man with a rifle had been bumped and jostled by the sudden struggle. His gun went off, spraying the air with bullets.

Anderson capitalized on the moment of confusion and lunged at the second man. Baxter ran to the area where she had thrown her gun and was searching desperately for it. Cory, after the initial surprise at Benjamin's quick move, jumped to help Benjamin. The first man's rifle fired three times. Bullets hit a column.

Other shots were fired. Baxter screamed in a shrill voice, "Everybody freeze!" She had found her gun and aimed it at the struggling men. She fired it just over their heads. "Stop it. Drop the guns!"

The men ceased their fierce but brief struggle over the rifles. All eyes were on Baxter. She moved her gun back and forth slowly. She had a grim look on her face. Her eyes were fierce.

Anderson had a graze wound in his scalp, and a trickle of blood oozed down behind his left ear and onto his neck. The first man had a bloody lip and a cut under his right eye. As hands relaxed on the rifles, Benjamin said, "Good work, Baxter." He attempted to pull the rifle from his opponent's hands but met resistance. The man smiled and held firmly to the gun. Cory had released his grip on the other man and his gun. He took a step to the side to get a clearer look at Baxter.

"Freeze, Mr. Cory," she ordered.

"What?"

Anderson and Benjamin looked oddly at the woman and let go of the rifles that the other men held onto.

"What do you mean?" Cory asked.

"Shut up!" commanded the first man. "She's with us, you fool." Cory could hardly believe what he heard.

"Baxter, why?" asked Anderson as he and the other men were motioned into a line.

"Money. They will give me a large share of the money exchanged for the technology," Baxter responded coldly.

The men with the guns grinned broadly and held Anderson, Benjamin, and Cory in position at gunpoint.

"Then you are responsible for those men knowing I had the watch and their running me off the road," Cory blurted out.

"Yes."

"But why didn't you just give them the watch in the first place?" asked Cory.

"I'll tell you why, Mr. Cory," Anderson answered. "I was with her when she opened the package containing the watch, and I was always near her from then until now."

"That's right," added Baxter. "I would not have had to reveal my association with the PF terrorist group if Benjamin wouldn't have been so quick to grab the gun a few minutes ago either. I had to guarantee my payment by being sure the PF had the chip."

"And you used me to help recover it here at the ruins," added Cory.

"Yes, Mr. Cory, you came in very handy. And it's ironic that it all happened here. I never dreamed that in my original instructions to you that I had named the actual place where we would find the chip," Baxter stated.

"Old Angela. You are partly responsible for her death," added Cory.

"I'm sorry about her, Mr. Cory. That was an accident. And she did prevent us from finding the chip with the help of the witches," Baxter said.

"Cut the talk," snarled the first terrorist. "Carl, rip that radio out of their car and slash the tires."

The second terrorist went over to the pickup, reached under the seat, and produced a knife. He then yanked the radio wires from the car and proceeded to cut the tires. As he was doing this, Anderson appealed to Baxter, "You know what they are going to do, don't you? They're going to kill us right here."

"Shut up!" shouted the first terrorist. He took a step toward Anderson.

"And what are they going to do at the nuclear power plant?" exclaimed Cory.

"I said to keep your mouths shut!" the terrorist yelled. He raised the rifle menacingly.

Baxter looked anxiously at the first terrorist and said, "It's not true. You're not going to shoot them, are you, Ronnie?"

"Don't worry about them, woman," he responded. "You're going to be taken care of with all that money. Carl had completed his task with the tires and now stood between Ronnie and Baxter.

"You three will like what I'm going to tell you now. Ha! Ha! Ha! That nuclear power station over there at Grand Gulf is just what the PF needs to gain attention and support for our cause. It'll make a pretty big fireball in the night; and when we claim credit for the destruction of it and its capitalistic exploiters, we'll get international attention," proclaimed Ronnie.

"Do you know what you're doing? Hundreds of thousands—millions of people—will be affected," Cory said.

"You're crazy," added Benjamin.

Ronnie just laughed.

"You said nobody would be hurt," Baxter said emphatically. "You said you wouldn't really damage the power plant, just hold some hostages and threaten to blow it up."

"Don't worry," Ronnie said coolly. "Enough talk. Carl, are you ready?"

"Yeah," he said as he raised his automatic rifle. "Let's do it." There was an awful moment of silence. Then the wind gusted all around them, making an eerie whistling noise through the tops of the columns.

Cory stared at Baxter. Her eyes were cold and harsh. He saw her take a small step backward that was unnoticed by the two terrorists. He heard the first ugly report of Ronnie's weapon and from the corner of his eye saw Anderson jerk and crumple to the ground. He saw a flash from Baxter's handgun and her lunge into Carl.

Both Cory and Benjamin rushed the two terrorists. Carl's rifle fired wildly off target, and Ronnie jerked his gun upward in pain after Anderson was hit. Cory yanked Ronnie's rifle away from him as he fell on the grassy open area among the columns.

Baxter was knocked down by the struggle for the gun. Each man twisted and pulled the gun, trying to wrest it from the control of the other. The men stumbled and fell to the ground—the gun between them. One of them squeezed the trigger. Bullets slashed through the air. The men were still. The terrorist was on top.

Cory, in the meantime, had picked up the other rifle and aimed it at the men. Cory and Baxter saw no movement for what seemed too long. Their eyes trained to detect a movement from the bodies.

The terrorist rolled off. His face, or what was left of it, was covered with blood. "My God!" exclaimed Baxter.

Cory rushed over to Lee Benjamin. Benjamin sat up slowly. He said, "The poor, crazy fool pulled the trigger and blew his chin and face away." Benjamin was wiping blood off himself.

Baxter turned to the other terrorist. "He's still alive!"

Cory and Benjamin moved over to them. Benjamin cradled the man's head in his arm. The terrorist opened his eyes. He looked at them and said weakly but haughtily, "You can't stop us. Not even now. The power plant will be in our control by midnight. The world will know what the People's Faction can do by morning. A giant fireball will signal our victory." His throat rasped. He took a weak breath, his final one.

"We must try to stop the other terrorists! Check Anderson!" shouted Benjamin after a moment of stunned silence.

Cory felt Anderson's pulse. Nothing. "It's too late for our friend." Baxter broke into tears. She sobbed loudly. "It's my fault for being so greedy! It's my fault!"

"Come on!" shouted Cory as he pulled her into the truck. Benjamin had found the keys in the ignition and cranked the engine. They sped away, leaving the silent bodies there with the now silent columns.

"The Wormwood Star," said Cory. "The bad thing Angela warned me of could happen tonight. How can they be stopped?"

"I don't know," replied Benjamin, "but we must try. Maybe the others aren't the fanatics these seemed to be, and we can talk them out of it. God help us if we can't!"

It was dark by the time they drove into Port Gibson and up to the sheriff's department office. Benjamin rapidly explained the situation to the local authorities and then called his district office while the Mississippi State Police were being summoned by the local department.

During this time sheriff department units were being sent to the Grand Gulf Power Plant. Just as the radio dispatcher had finished directing his next-to-last local unit, the telephone rang. It was security at Grand Gulf. The terrorists were already there, and assistance was being urgently requested.

Benjamin, Cory, and Baxter, and a deputy named Josh climbed in the only sheriff's car there and headed up Highway 61 to the turn-off to the nuclear power station as fast as possible.

After turning off on Grand Gulf Road, they went a little more than five miles to the access road to Unit One at the nuclear power plant. The huge cooling tower caught Cory's attention first. Then his eyes scanned the high-tension lines, towers, and poles and lighted buildings and areas of the complex. The whole setting was a field of flashing red and blue lights from the local and state police cars.

They pulled up to the line of police cars and got out cautiously because they could see the law officers and others crouched behind cars. Benjamin went ahead. He talked with a state trooper and what looked like the county sheriff.

In a few minutes he came back to them. He said, "Here's the situation. As you can see, there are three vehicles near the cooling tower. One of them is a power plant truck. The terrorists came up in a van and a car. They broke through the gate and were on their way to the building complex, but they were detoured by a fast-thinking security guard in a truck. Apparently, he saw their breakthrough at the gate and swerved so they would broadside his truck with their car. The van, trying to avoid a crash also, turned so sharply that it flipped over. Security approached the vehicles but were driven back by automatic weapon fire. They probably have automatic rifles like the two we encountered. The best guess is that there are about seven of them. We'll be better able to tell when we can get more lights on them. Right now there is little danger that we can tell to the power plant itself, but the terrorists may have the explosives and weapons that can change things. Some of them must have been hurt by the crash. That must be why no one has moved from the vehicles."

"What can we do to help?" asked Cory.

"Not much. A SWAT team is on its way from the state police. Unless they try to move, we have them boxed in for the moment. None of them have . . . "

A loud female voice stopped Benjamin in mid-sentence. He moved back to where the state troopers were. The voice cried out again, "You pigs listen out there! You pigs listen to me!" There was a silence.

"We are the People's Faction. Know our name. People's Faction." Another pause. "This whole nuclear power plant is going up in one great, big fireball! Do you hear? A huge fireball!"

The words rang out over the complex and died ominously away. Benjamin and the state trooper were about to use a bullhorn to talk when automatic rifle fire erupted from the van, sending bullets pelting the police cars. Police and security guards returned fire.

"They're pinned down," said Cory to Baxter. The shooting subsided. Everyone waited. No movement or sound from the terrorists.

Twice during the long night the terrorists fired their weapons at the encirclement of police and security personnel as if to let everyone know they were still there and still defiant.

Reporters and television cameras showed up but were kept at a distance. The SWAT team came and got into position. Other federal agents arrived, and Benjamin briefed them.

Daylight was about an hour away. A car engine cranked. Suddenly a trooper cried out, "They're making a move!" Shots rang out and grew in number and volume. Five people scattered from the van and zigzagged toward the buildings.

The car that had crashed into the truck had been started and backed away from it. Whoever was driving it steered it awkwardly toward the heaviest concentration of police. The driver gunned it and smashed into the police vehicles despite the heavy gunfire it drew.

At the same time the five figures running toward the building complex fired their guns over the range of buildings. Two were cut down by police bullets. The three others ran frantically onward. Another fell.

This time there was a bright flash and a small explosion and its resulting noise.

"He must have had explosives on him that he detonated," said Cory.

Another figure stumbled and fell. Only one remained running. Cory stood erect and watched the solitary figure. He couldn't tell much, even in the plant's lighting at that distance. He wondered why all of this was happening—why people would do such things.

He saw the figure jerk its arms upward. The next instant a bright flash and flame enshrouded the figure. He heard the noise of the explosion. He prayed that the terrorist had not gotten close enough to damage any delicate or sensitive part of the complex so that no radioactivity of any kind would be released.

Silence. No one moved momentarily. Then suddenly it seemed everyone but Cory and Baxter were running out here. She looked at him sadly and said, "I guess it's over." She handed him the computer chip. "I'm sorry, Mr. Cory." She slumped down against a police car.

Duane Cory watched her for a few seconds and then turned to walk away, out beyond most of the lights. He thought of old Angela.

He walked through the plant's gate and glanced up at the night sky. He heard more sirens and looked back at the complex. The cooling tower was his focus point. Above it in the sky he could see one star distinctly. "Wormwood Star. Wormwood Star," he thought. "Not tonight, old Angela, not tonight," he said aloud. "The third angel didn't blow his horn against us yet."

E-MAIL TO: Emily, Robbyn, Michelle, Melissa, Nicole, Katie, Corinna, Renae, Cindy, Aaron, Jami, Ashley, Melanie, Samantha, Michelle, and Melissa

Thank you again for the dinner, gift card, and kind thoughts you gave me on the last evening of EDU 445.

As I had said that evening we had dinner together to celebrate your program completion and graduation, the poem "Ulysses" by Alfred, Lord Tennyson came to my mind when you turned the celebration spotlight on me. Your compliments to me as a teacher vividly enliven and personalize the line, "I am part of all that I have met." For me as a teacher the line evokes two avenues of thought.

The first is that as a teacher I advised you, mentored you, instructed you, taught you, challenged you, frustrated you, consoled you, developed you, molded you, and fashioned you to one degree or another into the teacher you are now. Remember my example metaphor of a teacher being the sculptor who "finds Connie in the rock." I have helped "sculpt" each of you from "the marble block" that you were, so to speak, at the beginning of the teacher preparation program. I invested part of my teacher heart and soul and passion in each of you. Some of you I had more time to chisel and chip away at, and a few of you I had hardly any time to work with. But I feel that I am part of each of you as far as your teacher professional identity is concerned. You will carry some aspect or imprint of Dr. Smith forward with you into your teaching life whether you like it or not. I express my thanks and appreciation to you for that opportunity and hope I have served you well.

The second venue of thought is generated by the reciprocity that I interpret in the poetic line. If I am a part of you, then you are a part of me as well. I consider all of you as part of my extended teacher family. I learn from my students—from each of you. You helped "to sculpt" me into a better teacher. I am a life-long learner and a reflective practitioner who is constantly seeking to improve.

So, you understand that you as a group and as individuals really gave me three gifts that evening—the gift card with dinner, the gift of allowing me to be part of you, and the gift of your being part of me. I sincerely thank you for all the gifts—especially the last two. The last two gifts are great treasures. Thank you. You make this teacher extremely happy and fulfilled. As has been stated by others over the ages, teaching is the greatest profession because teaching creates all other professions. Please live up to that legacy. Returning to the last line of the poem "Ulysses," I encourage you personally and professionally to be ". . . strong in will/To strive, to seek, to find, and not to yield."

Dr. Smith

The Great Orthodontic Train Robbery

(inspired by story starter idea by Jim Smilie in the *Alexandria Daily Town Talk*, July 22, 1988)

Rich and renowned Boston dentist Percival Fauntleroy
Had in his mind that he looked a mere premolar boy
"A man I must be. I have to prove it to me."
Was what he said over and over just to see
If his body would answer his dry mouth's plea.

The advice of "Go West, young man!" he would heed
An opportunity to prove denticulation manhood he would need.
Fauntleroy closed his dental office all the while to proclaim
That dentigerous manhood he was really going to claim
With that implant in mind he boarded a San Francisco-bound train.

Somewhere in the Wild West the chugging train did lurch and jerk
To a stop to be boarded by robbers, each with halitosis and a smirk.
The leader of the Grinder Gang lowered his bandanna for all to see
But particularly and especially for the lovely and voluptuous ladies three.
He swaggered and announced with a bucktooth grin his name was C. C.

All eyes centered on C. C. with his fiery red beard and headful of unruly
    bright red hair.
C. C. smiled, winked, made goo-goo eyes, gave come-hither looks, all
    with a coquettish flare.
The leader of the gang, while the others leveled guns, flirted with the
    lovely women in dresses
By walking about, smiling to flash a gold crown, and gently tugging
    bountiful tresses.
Women flirted back, as Fauntleroy pondered the tough, manly qualities
    the robber possesses.

As C. C. moved about to each of the ladies and caressed each face and on each a kiss he placed,
His fellow robbers, taking watches, rings, currency, coins, necklaces— all the while they raced.
The gang with their new-stolen riches quickly took their loot and disembarked from the train,
But, of course, C. C. made a toothy grand exit from the ladies that was anything but plain.
Fauntleroy, sitting there grinding his teeth, wondered and pondered with his manly brain.

The boyish Boston dentist departed the train at the next station to achieve his manly goal.
He knew he must create a new Western legend whose amalgam deeds were yet untold.
He assembled his own jawsmith gang to be led by himself with a new legendary name
The Doc Plaque Gang would enter, compete, and win the train fame name game.
The art of train robbery would bridge new heights and would never be the same.

"Bicuspid!" exclaimed dentist Percival Fauntleroy, the soon-to-be dental train robber.
"When old train robber gangs learn of our exploits, all they will be able to do is slobber!"
Doc Plaque devised a brilliant train robbery plan that would certainly pulp fiction ensure
That the Doc Plaque Gang, filling all of its legend's expectations, would definitely endure.
That Doc Plaque would become known as a manly man. "Bicuspid! It was for sure!"

The gang Doc Plaque pulled together were not yet men of fame or even honorable mention.
They were Gene Ist, Oral Robbins, Pio Rhea, and, of course, the Doc of that boyish detention.
Drifter Gene Ist, constantly toking on roll-your-own tumble weed cigarettes, was always high.
Oral Robbins, an out-of-luck, snaggle-toothed street preacher, was another one that drew nigh.
Pio Rhea, unemployed Mexican chef and Tequila brew meister, joined with an enameled sigh.

Even though he always took a toke, high Gene Ist was the Doc's right-hand nitrous oxide man,
And so Doc Plaque and Gene Ist did develop a great manly and legendary train robbery plan.
Doc, along with his right-hand man, explained the robbery plan and its orthodontia rationale.
The planners looked at the other dreamers and promised money for each and every Doc pal.
They would pull the job as the train slowed to cross the decaying bridge over the Root Canal.

The gang desired currency and jewelry and coins; those items were all on the collective brain.
Said Oral, "I would give all my wisdom teeth if them crown jewels was on that thar train."
But for Doc Plaque saying the money was the crowning glory was just a paltry fabrication.
Because for the Doc, money was just an aside, and this first criminal act sets the foundation,
And the actual event with the ladies swooning would proclaim loudly his manhood declaration.

The old decaying Root Canal bridge design reminded Doc of his latest orthodontic training.
Doc thought the bridgework design a very good sign, and the gang showed no complaining.
Doc visualized the passenger and robber interaction that would yield desired manly abstraction.
But he knew that once the criminal infraction gained necessary traction to cause counteraction,
It would produce for him redaction of his boyish exaction and growth of his manly satisfaction.

The chugging train approached the orthodontic-structured bridge. As if on cue, it did slow.
Three of the gang were nervous, but not the Doc. The gang leader shouted, "Bicuspid, go!"
Before the turn as the train went slow, the gang spurred its horses and to the train drew nigh.
Pio and Oral galloped ahead to the locomotive and ordered the engineer to stop with a loud cry.
Doc and Gene moved to the passenger car, jumped on at opposite ends, and yelled to the sky.

Bursting through the doors in an instant, Doc, instead of pulling molars, pulled his gun.
Gene menacingly waved his double-barrel around; all passengers raised hands in unison.
An older male passenger, clutching his travel satchel, begged the outlaw gang not to shoot.
Doc bravely and quickly responded, "Open your mouth again, and I'll drill ya, ya old coot!"
Gene blasted the roof with a single barrel and then puffed away at his tumbleweed cheroot.

In his weed-clouded mind, Gene was now the legendary "high" plains drifter of dime novels.
Pio and Oral in the locomotive felt power in guns and would never again be one who grovels.
But the transformation of a boyish man to a manly man was taking place in Doc the legendary.
Because he had not shaved in weeks, his face had become quite hairy and really sort of scary.
Percival was a different carie-free man; he was the beneficiary of his own heroic commentary.

The passenger car was his stage, and he was the acclaimed Shakespearean actor of renown.
The passengers were his captive audience; each woman an adorer; each man a mere clown.
All eyes and all ears were on the main performer, the enamel star—the one, the only Doc Plaque.
Doc, his manhood now alive and intact, decided that with the beautiful women he would interact.
He pranced up and down the aisle and winked and smiled and all kinds of flirtation did transact.

When Doc Plaque brandished his Colt .45 all around, the men thought he could not be disarmed.
All of the women—beautiful and not so—were mesmerized by Doc, not accidentally, charmed.
What the men did not know was that each cartridge chamber of the Colt .45 was only a cavity
Because Doc Plaque in all his excitement for the train robbery with all of its intense gravity,
Had forgotten to load the Colt .45 before beginning his ascent into his manhood of depravity.

He twirled to shout to the amalgam of men passengers, and with firm-set jaw he yelled out:
"You thumb sucker! You human abscess! You dry socket! You canker sore! You sauerkraut!"
The good doctor now dutifully again turned his attention and charm to the women in a rush.
The beautiful ladies blushed at Doc's manly antics, and sexy Flossy in a swoon did gush,
"If only he would bathe, brush his teeth, and get decent clothes . . . " Now Doc said, "Hush!"

"Pardon me, ladies," Doc said to all the women passengers, "but I have an inlay job to do here."
So Doc in a manly amble and with a Don Juan outlook advanced in this passenger car to its rear.
Now Doc Plaque with the confidence of the legendary lover produced a flirtation comprehensive.
Doc kissed lips, held hands, touched cheeks, waxed romantic but did not purloin to be offensive.
For unlike an impacted tooth, this train robbery for the passengers proved quite inexpensive.

Bicuspid! Doc had not forgotten to clean them out, for that procedure was not his prime intent.
Remember that his goal was to capture his manhood and prove it to all with legendary content.
He wanted all the passengers to leave the train at the next station with the legend of Doc Plaque.
He knew his gang in its giddy state would notice lack of loot at the hideout when they got back.
Doc, a rich man, previously placed bags of his money and dental fringe benefits there in a stack.

Doc signaled his gang to release its control on the train, now completed
 his robbery reputation.
"This is Doc Plaque Gang territory, and all other train robbers keep out!"
 was his declaration.
All this was the manly stuff that Western legends are made of, at least in
 Doc's human brain.
The fear and loathing of the Tartar of the West, no longer the boy dentist,
 would forever remain.
Doc, now transcendental and with newly receding gums, extracted
 himself nicely from the train.

(This poem was a revision to my prose entry into the newspaper writing contest to finish the story starter.)

Writing History

Was it some historian who said "The public be damned!" when it comes to reading history? The general public may very well believe so because it seems historians think history should be studied, written, and read in scholarly academic settings by Ph. D.s who study and write for other Ph. D.s to read. Historians have tended to write for each other and not for a generally educated audience. They have withdrawn to college and university enclaves and rarely come out. They grasp for that "noble dream" of objectivity and true history. They have abandoned history in the public schools to the educationalists.

Historians ponder the question of how to get more people to read history. "Why history?" and "Why study history?" are the questions in the minds of those outside the discipline. Theodore Hamerow says "the most common argument advanced in defense of historical learning has been that it can teach society to make more rational decisions about actions to be taken or policies to be pursued." The generally educated public would agree, but this public will not read "dry-as-dust" monographs that cause only a history Ph. D.'s heart to palpitate. If the public does not read, the utilitarian value of history books becomes nil.

Carl Becker in his 1931 presidential address to the American Historical Association argued "the scholar must adapt his learning to the needs and interests of 'Mr. Everyman,' the broad general public, whose support is essential for the continuing vitality of historiography." He further stated "history that lies inert in unread books does no work in the world."

Historians must break away from the narrow confines of the university campus to broaden their vision while keeping true to the objectivism of historic fact. They need to write for the educated public as well as themselves. They need to wrest the study of history in the elementary and secondary schools away from the educationalists and to inject living, breathing, exciting history into the classroom.

I agree with Hamerow who says historians must "write better" and "master the techniques of the social sciences," remembering that historical "roots lie deep in the literary tradition of our civilization," and that historians "should learn to count and quantify without severing our ties to the humanities." I believe an amalgamation of science and art is required. Narrative history within the bounds of objectivity is the avenue to reach the educated public.

Some historians have already returned to traditional narrative style because scientific history has failed to deliver the goods. Thinking of history as a branch of literature may flavor the writing of history enough to entice a large readership. Francis Parkman and other romantic historians thought of history in this manner. To them, history was an art—not a cold scientific compilation of facts and theories. But literary effectiveness should never circumvent objectivity and authenticity. The essentialness of objectivity precludes a resurrection of romantic history. But practicing historians must veer away from monographic studies and writing styles which more often than not run counter to any literary style. Revisionism in historians' writing styles must occur just as revisionism occurs in historiography itself. The public awaits.

Contest Entry (that did not win)

If this contest "gifts" the person I nominate in the manner I suggest, not a single penny of the contest award will be directly spent on the person nominated. This condition would be to her liking. Her gift would the presence of relatives and friends surrounding her at her fiftieth wedding anniversary. The contest award money would be spent to provide travel and lodging for these other persons.

She is only five feet two inches tall at most. She is an unassuming, diminutive Southern girl. Her name does not appear in the newspapers or on television. It will not be in any spotlight and does not draw public attention. These facts are to her liking as well. What she does, she does not do for reward or notoriety because that is not in her nature. She knows nothing else.

The person I want "to gift" grew up poor. She has memories of living in a house with no running water, watching her mother make her a dress out of a flour sack, and chopping weeds in a cotton field to help her family earn extra money in order to get by. Perhaps that is why she is such a giving, generous person. She knows what it is to have little or nothing when it comes to material possessions. She worked at a department store to help put me through undergraduate school when we were first married. For many years we struggled financially on a beginning Louisiana teacher's salary. When my mother was diagnosed with pancreatic/liver cancer, my wife went back to work as a substitute teacher. She gave of herself to every student in that role, while earning extra money to assist in caring for her beloved, cancer-stricken mother-in-law. But her generosity with the little money we had after paying bills was not the real measure of her giving to others. She gave something greater than money. I observed her compassion and love unselfishly given as she passed it on to "our" dying mother. Her tender touch was evident as she helped her dress and cook and serve her food. The grasping of a weak hand, the kind words spoken to encourage, the gentle yet loving hug and the kiss on the sallow cheek—all were gifts freely and tenderly given. This giving is the real person she is.

Her real gift to relatives and others is the gift of herself—the extra attention paid to her children and those of others, the patience to parents, her smile, her kind word, her "going the extra mile," her caring, her humanity, her genuine interest. I have experienced this wonderful, giving woman all our married life.

All of the above reasons and more are why I wish "to gift" her on our fiftieth wedding anniversary in August 2018. We have already saved money for the two of us to celebrate our fiftieth anniversary in Disney World in less than two years. Our two children and their spouses plus our two grandsons will be there. But I want her to have a greater circle of family and close friends there as well; the problem is that most of our family members are unable to afford to go to be with us for the special time. I wish to have family there who can not pay their own way. Having more than just the immediate family there with us would be an extra special gift for my wife!

The "gift of family" being there at our fiftieth wedding anniversary celebration is the best gift I could ever give her. This gift for her—spending the contest award dollars on others—is not merely a great gift for her but a greater gift for many others, a gift of memories forever folded into a fiftieth wedding anniversary celebration.

The End of
The Ó Súilleabháin Manuscripts

Plans for Another in the Works!

ABOUT THE AUTHOR

Dr. Thomas S. Smith, Sr., is a retired educator who served in the Avoyelles Parish (LA) public school system for 33 years. During his tenure there, he served as a high school teacher of English and social studies at Hessmer High School, assistant principal at Hessmer High School, assistant principal at Bunkie High School, assistant principal at Riverside Elementary School, principal at Lafargue High School, principal at Bunkie Middle School, and English/Social Studies Resource Teacher/Grants Coordinator in the district office. He worked as adjunct faculty for Northwestern State University of Louisiana, Central Texas College, Louisiana State University at Alexandria, Macomb Community College (MI), Baker College of Auburn Hills (MI), Baker College of Clinton Township (MI), and University of Phoenix—Metro Detroit. He taught as full-time faculty for seven years at Baker College of Auburn Hills (MI), where he taught education, history, and geography courses as well as serving as a supervisor for student teachers. He holds a BA from the University of Louisiana at Monroe, a MEd from Louisiana State University at Baton Rouge, a MA from Louisiana State University at Baton Rouge, and a PhD from the University of New Orleans. He also earned more than 50 additional graduate hours. He is the author of the *Just a Piece of Red String* historical fiction novel series.

Made in the USA
Columbia, SC
02 November 2023